MW01632865

The Maverick Millionaire

Wealth Advice from one of America's Youngest Self-Made Millionaires

Jordan Wirsz

CEO, Diamond Bay Investments

Palari Publishing LLP
Richmond, Virginia

The Maverick Millionaire© 2007, By Jordan Wirsz

Published by Palari Publishing
www.palaribooks.com

All rights reserved. No part of this book may be reproduced or utilized in any form or by any means, electronic or mechanical, including photocopying, recording or by any information storage and retrieval system, without permission in writing from the Publisher.

Inquiries should be addressed to: Permissions Department
Palari Publishing LLP, 1113 W. Main St., Richmond, VA 23220

Library of Congress Cataloging-in-Publication Data

Wirsz, Jordan, 1983-
The maverick millionaire : wealth advice from one of America's youngest self-made millionaires / Jordan Wirsz.
p. cm.
ISBN-13: 978-1-928662-08-2 (hardcover)
ISBN-10: 1-928662-08-0 (hardcover)
1. Success in business. 2. Success—Psychological aspects. 3. Millionaires. 4. Wirsz, Jordan, 1983- I. Title.
HF5386.W598 2007
658.4'09—dc22

2007009370

Printed in the United States of America
10 9 8 7 6 5 4 3 2 1

Cover design: Ted Randler
Interior: Brian Bear
Consulting Editor: Marcus Webb

"The attainment of success is outwardly assured, when we are inwardly matured... When a fact is fully realized on the spiritual level, then what remains is merely to carry out our task on the physical level, and that is foreordained... By mastering our inner resources, the thing is accomplished already."

— Ralph Waldo Emerson

"As a man thinketh in his heart, so is he."

— Proverbs, Chapter 23, verse 7.

(The Maverick Millionaire™ Plan

There are four phases to the **REBL Plan**:

1. **R**eview your goals
2. **E**valuate your plan
3. **B**uild your wealth
4. **L**everage your successes)

As you go through this plan, apply the tools and techniques in each level to your own situation and your own dreams. With a lot of work and determination, you will ultimately become a true Maverick Millionaire™.

Maverick Moment ('mav-rik 'mO-ment), noun:

1: an inspirational story that demonstrates the power of dreams and determination

2: an activity that applies to your own specific interests

Maverick Motivator ('mav-rik mo ti•va tor'), noun:

1: statistics or facts that demonstrate the importance of taking control of your career

2: use these facts as a way to stay focused

Table of Contents

Phase I:

REVIEW Your Maverick Goals

Remember, a Maverick Moment is an inspirational story that demonstrates the power of your own specific dreams and determination.

Flying riveted my attention from the time I was 5 years old. We lived on the side of a hill and I would see airplanes and helicopters flying all over the valley.

I loved to see them in the sky.

I can remember daydreaming, even at that age, about being a pilot and flying around myself. Kids have vivid imaginations, and I could "see" myself at the stick, zooming through the air, banking and turning, diving and climbing...gazing down at the world from the commanding perspective of a bird.

It drove me crazy that I wasn't up there with them!

I started bugging my mom about it. Every day. Day after day. "Mom, I want to go fly! I want to fly airplanes!" Finally after a few months, she drove me to the Redlands Airport. We talked to one of the guys running the fuel sales office.

He said, "I've got a plane. Would you like to go for a ride?"

Minutes later I was strapped into the back seat of a Cessna 182 high-wing monoplane. We zipped down the runway and then –oh, my gosh–we're up in the air! The windows are so high that I have to strain to see over the door panels. Outside, the atmosphere is so hazy that you can't see any great distance. But I don't care. I'M FLYING!!!

We did one square pattern over the airport, barely 10 minutes in the air–if that. We landed and I climbed out wearing a three-day grin...

Who says dreams can't come true?

Chapter 1:

The Single Greatest Factor in Success

In my opinion, a book on success should start by telling you from chapter one, sentence one, how to be successful–so I'll jump right in by saying *the single most important factor in becoming wealthy, healthy, and happy is that you must believe that it can be done.*

And, even more importantly, you must believe that YOU can do it.

On first hearing, this may sound simple–even simplistic. It is neither. Believing in the possibility of your own success is not simple, because we're all bombarded, day and night, with a relentless onslaught of negative messages.

"You can't win." *"They'* won't give you a chance." "The system is rigged." "It's not what you know; it's who you know." "Happiness is for other people–not for you." "Who are YOU to think you can succeed where so many others (and betters) have tried and failed?"

Other negative messages include: "You don't have the right skills." "You don't have the right credentials." "You're a member of the wrong race." "You're a member of the wrong class." "You come from the wrong place on the map."

And then there are these old reliables: "You haven't paid your dues." "You haven't suffered enough, worked enough, sweated enough." "Everything has come too easily for you–you're *too* perfect." "Everything is too hard for you–you're damaged goods." "You're just unlucky." "You're not smart enough." "You're not pretty enough." "You don't know enough." "You're not old enough." "You're not *young* enough." "You're not *anything* enough."

And so on...the list is infinite. We get these messages from our parents, our friends, our teachers, our coaches, our colleagues, and from perfect strangers. We get them from TV, movies, music, magazines, books, newspapers, and the Internet. What's worse, we also carry these negative notions around inside our own heads–even if we don't always consciously realize it. Overcoming this relentless drumbeat of negativity is neither simple nor easy. But it can be done. This book will teach you how to do it.

The Connection between Believing and Achieving

Also, the statement that "success begins with belief" is not simplistic. On the contrary: the connection between *faith* (what we truly believe inside) and *achievement* (what we manifest outside) is one of the most mysterious dynamics in human life. It is also one of the most profound, and the most powerful.

This dynamic between faith and achievement has been a crucial subject of study and field of practice for years, including ancient philosophers and the founders of all the world's great religions. It also includes today's most successful business people, political leaders, sports stars, scientific geniuses, and cultural icons.

The purpose of this book is to show you how to master this powerful faith/achievement dynamic. I will teach you how to use it to realize the wealth, health, and happiness that you were meant to enjoy. So here is my most important, core principle for success:

If you desire to be "rich outside," first be "rich inside."

Yes, we're all aware that some people–far too many–possess material riches while manifesting internal poverty. However, my experience tells me it's much harder to build a solid foundation of wealth that way. I know for a fact that it's much harder for a spiritually impoverished person to hang onto material riches, too.

Finally, even if such a person does manage to hold onto their wealth, I am convinced they cannot enjoy it to the fullest. "For what does it profit a man if he shall gain the whole world, and lose his own soul?"

A Practical Guidebook to Your Success

The Maverick Millionaire™ principles are based on spiritual values, but they are also a pragmatic, hardheaded guideline to achieving real-world success...any kind of success.

Perhaps you wish to enjoy the American dream of material wealth and career achievement. Or maybe you're pursuing a social, moral, scientific, or artistic ideal of rewarding relationships and meaningful work. Or some combination of the above. But however you personally define YOUR success, the crucial preparation for it is the same.

You must begin by stocking your inner resources of mind, body, and soul with the right "capital"–the right principles and beliefs. In this book I will teach you how to discover those mental, spiritual, and physical resources within yourself, and in the world around you.

The second crucial step is that you must "leverage" that capital in your daily life with the right actions and the right strategies. I will teach you those actions and strategies, and I will explain how to use them to leverage your inner resources.

After that, it's up to you. I'll supply the knowledge; you supply the will and desire.

What Does "Success" Mean to You?

You also supply your personal definition of success. As I said, each of us has our own concept, our own dream of what success really means.

For me, success means a balanced life. For sure, I'm very enthusiastic about building a successful company and achieving substantial wealth–but I'm also passionate today about health and fitness; flying and other recreation; and making a contribution to my community and the world at large.

For you, success might be winning an Olympic Gold medal...getting your formal education...entering the medical field and saving lives...creating a magnificent symphony or painting...or even traveling to outer space!

However you define it, the *Maverick Millionaire* principles will empower you to achieve it...and to achieve it faster than you probably dreamed was possible.

Make no mistake; achieving wealth and happiness requires hard work. There are no shortcuts–but I will show you the most direct routes. Furthermore, even after you have achieved success, you must continue to be disciplined and hardworking, if you intend to *keep* the wealth that you have created.

But I can promise you one thing. If you follow the right road, applying yourself diligently and faithfully, you will discover that your work becomes as rewarding as it is challenging. And rewards will come to you on all levels: material, intellectual, emotional, and spiritual.

Best of all, when you achieve your success, you will know that you have truly earned it. You will be prepared to enjoy your success–and your life–to the fullest. You'll experience the unparalleled joy of being a *Maverick Millionaire.*

How do I know that YOU can do it? Because I've done it myself!

Chapter 2:

How I Become a Self-Made Multimillionaire at 22

In 2002 I quit my $22,000 a year job as a commercial pilot for a small executive air service based in Jacksonville, Florida. I tossed a few things in a battered suitcase and climbed into my beat-up 1994 Dodge Intrepid, a total clunker with a failing radiator.

"Intrepid" turned out to be a surprisingly good name for my vehicle. "Insanely Optimistic" might have been even better. As I drove through the steamy Southeast, and then across the deserts of the West, I was forced to keep the windows open and keep the heater on full-blast. This pulled heat away from the engine and prevented the radiator from boiling over.

After 2,500 hot dusty miles I arrived in Las Vegas, Nevada, on April Fool's Day.

Before I left Florida, some of my friends had made it clear who they thought the fool was: me. Was I out of my mind? Why give up a steady job and move more than halfway across the country to a town where I knew virtually no one?

Now that I was here amidst the neon and the sand, I wondered fleetingly if they might have been right. I was 19 years old. I had no house, uncertain job prospects, and just $7,000 in savings in my bank account. I owned five shirts, two pairs of pants, and two pairs of running shoes.

Today, I am the CEO of my own company, Diamond Bay Investments, with a net worth of many millions.

> MAVERICK MOTIVATOR:
>
> **Put down the video game!**
>
> (Bureau of Labor Statistics data for 2005 show that some 370,000 young people ages 16-24 were self-employed, the occupational category that includes entrepreneurs.)
>
> 

I Made My Money the Old-Fashioned Way. I Earned It!

I did not inherit, steal, or cheat my way into these riches. Nor did I "luck into" wealth and success. I earned it myself–every dollar. I planned, worked, and sacrificed for it. I sweated and dreamed for it. Since the age of four, my life's focus has been to become successful.

What motivated me? Perhaps it was seeing how my parents struggled financially during my childhood. I grew up in a single-parent household on the wrong side of the tracks. My mother claimed that she had once been a millionaire. To hear her tell it, although times were hard, her ship was always just about to come in, again.

The way I saw it, my mother, my sisters, and I were always on the verge of going under. I vowed that when I grew up, I would never permit myself to be in that situation.

Today my life is very different. Financial security stopped being an issue for me a couple of million dollars ago.

As for my personal life, I'll let the psychologists explain why a guy who grew up in an atmosphere of instability develops into a true romantic who idealizes close families. And, although I may spend long hours at the office most days, please don't think I'm just a drudge at a desk. I follow a vigorous and disciplined fitness program–weightlifting, treadmill runs, diet–to keep myself in tip-top physical shape.

I need to be in excellent condition because, for fun, on weekends I fly aerobatic routines in my Extra 300 L high-performance aircraft. Putting ten times normal earth gravity on your body leaves you bruised and battered, and it requires enormous physical strength to fly the plane under these conditions.

Sometimes my wild aerial maneuvers are executed at national air shows before crowds of 10,000 people. Having an audience certainly gives my flight an extra kick. But on most occasions, it's just me and my airplane up there, flying alone for the pure joy of it–performing maneuvers that birds never dreamed of.

As far as I'm concerned, there is no greater thrill than tumbling nose over tail during a gorgeous desert sunset. As your aircraft hurtles through the sky, you are experiencing the forces of several times earth gravity on your body. Meanwhile your engine is screaming like it's about to explode. And the entire planet appears to be turning somersaults two miles "above" your canopy. What an incredible high!

Work Hard, Work Smart, Work Honestly.

This is my life. I say all of this to illustrate a very important point:

- Success is **NOT** a matter of "paying your dues" for a specific number of years. I didn't!
- Success does **NOT** depend on climbing the organizational ladder. I didn't do that, either.
- And, although I've made my fortune in Las Vegas, success is absolutely **NOT** a result of luck, nor of buying the right lottery ticket, nor pulling a handle on a slot machine!

I went from doing just ok to multimillionaire statue in just under three years through my own hard work and determination...with the help of a superb team of colleagues at my company...and thanks to the invaluable guidance of three mentors.

One mentor taught me about life and about myself. A second mentor taught me a trade. My third mentor taught me to stop kidding myself, and put up or shut up. All of my mentors, colleagues, customers, employees, and even my competitors have shown me repeatedly that this is a balanced, action-reaction universe. What you get out of it is what you put into it. What you give to life, life gives back to you–multiplied.

Can you really get rich by following the Golden Rule–

"Do unto others as you would have them do unto you"?

Absolutely. In fact, in the long run, I don't believe you can profit from anything else!

Chapter 3:

The Secret of My Success... and Yours!

Many people who read this book are probably asking: "Okay, Jordan, specifically how did you do it? How did you go from a net worth of around $7,000 to being a millionaire in just a couple of years?" I'll answer that question briefly at the beginning of this chapter. As we go along, I'll give lots of detailed examples and specific lessons from my own story...starting with the fact that a decade of learning preceded that two years of effort.

But I don't want to dwell on autobiography first and foremost, because this is not a book about "how you can duplicate Jordan Wirsz's personal business history." The dynamic U.S. economy changes too quickly–and differences between regional markets are too great–for any one individual's step-by-step roadmap (including mine) to be applicable in all times and places. That's why I have little respect for "one size fits all," cookie-cutter, get-rich-quick schemes that are hawked all over the place.

At the same time, I firmly believe that my story contains some timeless principles that apply to anyone, anyplace, at any time. My experience offers universal lessons that apply to any goal, and to any definition of success. It is these principles and lessons that I want to teach you in this book, because I truly believe they are the most valuable for you–wherever your own journey to success may take you.

Three Crucial Turning Points

My own personal roadmap to success had three crucial turning points. *First was my decision to move to Las Vegas.* There is an old saying that "If you want to make money, you should go where the money is." Real estate, and specifically Las Vegas real estate, has been booming for at least 15 years.

For someone like me, whose definition of success includes achieving significant wealth at a young age– and who started his first business at the age of 13—-the combination of this city and this industry provided the ideal environment. I went to work in the mortgage lending field, and learned the financial side of this highly profitable business. This move also allowed me to meet two key mentors who taught me a lot about business in general, and about the real estate lending business in particular.

My first year in Las Vegas, I learned the mortgage lending trade from the ground up. During my first two months, my earnings were zero! Eventually I achieved the typical up-and-down, good-month / bad-month record of a reasonably successful loan officer. My second year in Vegas, I went beyond the basics and applied some marketing techniques that, while hardly revolutionary, were innovative for the field at that time. I hired a fulltime, experienced account rep to go out and get deals, while I concentrated on funding the deals that my rep brought in. This resulted in my steadily processing millions of dollars of business per month, and helped me earn a place at the top of the sales chart in one of the city's best mortgage lending firms.

The second crucial turning point in my roadmap to success was *my decision to launch my own business*. My company focuses on a specialized branch of the real estate finance market called "private money lending." Basically, private money lending means funding mortgages with private dollars from individual investors, rather than going through banks or other institutions to get the money. It also includes making private loans that use solid real estate as collateral, and large multimillion-dollar commercial deals nationwide. Private lenders have lots more room to maneuver regarding whom they lend to, what deals they fund, and how fast the deals can get done. Borrowers pay a premium interest rate to obtain the greater speed and flexibility that private investors/lenders can offer. So this private financing can be amazingly profitable.

I opened my company two years after I arrived in Las Vegas. I wasn't wealthy yet. But as the owner of my own company in a high-potential market, for the first time in my life I had a real shot at *becoming wealthy*. Was it a risk to launch my own outfit? Yes, although perhaps not as big a risk as it may have seemed. In a sense, opening my own company was like my original decision to move to Vegas. After all, if the move didn't work out, I could always go back to Florida and become a professional pilot again (which is what I was doing before). Similarly, if my own company didn't work out, I knew I could always get another job at another mortgage lending firm. So, if these were risks, they were calculated, reasonable ones.

The third crucial turning point on my roadmap to success came during my company's initial shakedown period. We began with many ups and downs...with lots of hiring (and some firing)...and with a promising, if uneven, revenue curve. But several months after launching the business, I realized that I was doing something fundamentally wrong. I was behaving almost as if I were still a lending officer at someone else's company, only now with more assistants. It was time to stop focusing on chasing deals and processing deals, in order to step back and think strategically about the company itself. In other words, I decided to *stop thinking like a mere "business owner" and start thinking–and acting–like a true CEO.*

I hired a key executive who was young, but she had a great work ethic and significant experience in the Vegas real estate field. Most important, her tremendous administrative and organizational talents perfectly complemented my big-picture vision and drive. She immediately added in-house loan servicing to our list of client services, which was a vital strength. She also began putting systems and procedures in place that were designed to make the company run like a well-oiled machine. Together, we built the company's key departments and hired the personnel to staff them.

I learned, through a steady process of trial and error, how to set the overall strategy; how to weld a collection of disparate individuals into a smoothly integrated team; how to give my staff authority over their jobs; how to encourage them to be results-oriented; and how get them to take responsibility for their roles in the company. I learned how to practice the fine art of "management by walking around," which means being hands-on without being "in your face."

Making the transition from a "business owner mentality" to the "CEO outlook" yielded dramatic results for the company. Exactly three years and one month after my arrival in Las Vegas with around $7,000 to my name–we were chalking up *monthly* revenues well into six figures.

The Ultimate Success Secret

Now, what can YOU learn from my personal story? Is the lesson that you should move to Las Vegas and open a real estate business? I seriously doubt it! Probably 99% of the people reading this book don't have a passion for real estate the way I did from the time I was 12 years old. (And anyway, I don't need the competition.)

One thing I hope you *will* learn from my story is the ultimate secret of success. You can read dozens of success books and talk to hundreds of successful people, and you will discover that every expert has a different answer. The key to success has been described as determination, planning, learning from failure, promoting innovation and creativity, mastering change, teamwork, leadership, taking strategic risks, and on and on.

All of these answers are true. In fact, there are dozens more principles that are equally true and equally important. But in my opinion, ONE secret lies at the core of all of these principles.

The ultimate secret of success, health, wealth, and happiness is:
DESIRE.

Of all the resources that make you a maverick millionaire, desire is the greatest strength that can help you become "maverick rich." And the wonderful thing is, it's a resource that you already have inside you. It's innate. Every person is born with a deep, inner dream...an ultimate vision of themselves and their life...a passionate enthusiasm for a certain field or activity, and a natural ability to do that thing well. The hard part, for some, is finding out exactly what your true desire really is. You must look within yourself with an honest, steady, searching eye, and you must be honest with yourself about what you find there.

If you truly know what your deepest desire is, you'll be willing to work hard to achieve your goal. You'll be passionate about learning everything there is to know about the subject. You'll discover, to your joy and amazement, that you have real talent for this area. You will experience fortunate coincidences. Doors will open that seem to indicate you were meant to work in this particular field or do this particular thing. Setbacks will only stimulate you to dig in and work harder. Achieving success will satisfy you temporarily. Then it will become a spur to aim even higher...do even more...go even farther.

If you don't recognize yourself in this picture, maybe it's time to reassess exactly where your passion really lies. If you hope to put the power of desire to work in your life, then you must first know what you really, really want. To me, this is a matter of being honest with ourselves...a matter of holding ourselves accountable. So another crucial secret of my success and yours is that you cannot succeed without being absolutely honest with yourself.

Such gut-level honesty and accountability are not always easy. Sometimes our self-concept is wrapped up in a version of ourselves that we "think" we want to become, or "believe" that we should be. But the truth is, deep down we don't really want to be that person or do that thing. Our reluctance to commit, and our unwillingness to act, proves it.

A classic example could be a young person whose parents want him or her to enter a certain profession. Some young people think through this issue for themselves, then make the decision to pursue that same goal on their own, which is great. Unfortunately, a certain percentage may unthinkingly adopt their parents' goal as their own without going through such a soul-searching process. They dutifully drag themselves through years of grad school and, if they complete it, they resign themselves to a lifelong career of passionless mediocrity and under-achievement. An even more common example is the person who says, "I want to get in shape," but never commits to the diet and exercise program that will achieve that result (or if he does commit, he isn't consistent). Yet another example is the person who says, "Someday I'll learn to play the piano," but somehow she never gets around to signing up for lessons.

Do these people really want what they claim to want? I say often they are kidding themselves with false dreams that are not their heart's desire. They waste time and energy going down the wrong road. By failing to be honest with themselves about their true desires, they are depriving themselves of any real chance to enjoy success.

Honesty, accountability, willingness to make sacrifices–however you look at it, it all comes back to the same thing. Desire! Desire is the *indispensable fuel* for success. Lack of desire is the ultimate reason for lack of success.

Success Is What YOU Make It

An important lesson that I hope you might learn from my story is that "Success is what you make it." Each of us must define our own yardstick for success. And we have to make it happen in our own life.

My own success has grown from a combination of circumstances, personality traits, individual relationships, unusual experiences, and many other factors that are as unique to me as my fingerprints. I don't believe anyone could deliberately copy my life's journey to success. *Your success will be equally as unique to you, as mine is to me…and as every successful person's is to them.*

To me, running your own company is the most fun you can have in a career. I started my first company when I was 12, selling health products. Naturally, I am a great admirer of successful, self-made business people, from Bill Gates and Donald Trump to Martha Stewart and Mary Kay. But I also admire successful individuals in many other fields: science, academics, government, sports, the arts, public service.

With so many choices, each of us needs to ask ourselves: what does success really mean to ME? There are as many valid definitions of success as there are individuals on this planet. What counts is: what is important to YOU in YOUR life? It is an intensely personal question. Nobody can tell you what you should be successful at, how to define your personal success, or how to measure it.

Another way to express all of this is to say that the secret of your success is YOU: knowing yourself; being honest with yourself; and focusing on your unique personal desires, abilities, and talents...the things that make you "maverick rich." YOU are your single greatest resource. If you can bring your true strengths to bear, you will create your own one-of-kind roadmap to achievement...

And I guarantee you that YOU WILL BE A SUCCESS!

Chapter 4:

Wealth Is A Choice!

If You Want To Become Wealthy, Exercise Your Power to Choose

For the vast majority of people who live on this planet, wealth does not happen by accident. Now of course, it's certainly true that in the case of inherited wealth, some people do find themselves wealthy through no effort of their own. But that wasn't me, and since you're reading this book, I'm guessing that's probably not you, either.

There are certain people in this world who are fortunate enough to get extremely wealthy by pursuing their passion in a field that, in and of itself, has little or nothing to do with money. Physical skill in kicking a soccer ball or putting a golf ball has no inherent connection with money, but David Beckham and Tiger Woods became wealthy as a byproduct of developing their athletic prowess in these respective areas. (Although in Woods' case, it's pretty clear that Tiger and his parents had their eyes on those million-dollar purses all along.)

Oprah Winfrey and Steven Spielberg are both super-wealthy, but they did not make wealth their top priority, either. Like Beckham and Woods, they also became wealthy as a byproduct of pursuing excellence in their respective fields–in this case, broadcasting and filmmaking.

(It's wonderful to become wealthy while pursuing your dreams in sports, the arts, entertainment, journalism, saving the planet, or what have you; and I am the first to applaud everyone who can do that. But despite the Davids, Tigers, Oprahs, and Spielbergs of this world, such an indirect method is (ordinarily) not the fastest, surest way to wealth for most of us.

Imprint this fact permanently on your brain's memory cells: 999 times out of 1000, people become wealthy because they decide, first and foremost, to aim DIRECTLY at that outcome.)

Follow The Money.
Eventually, the Money Will Follow You.

Most people who become millionaires enter a business, or create one, where rivers of money are already flowing. They do so with the intention of working hard to ensure that their products or services offer excellence, knowing that if they create enough excellence, they will attract a healthy stream of that "river of money" to flow into their own pockets.

And, by golly, that is exactly what happens.

This is not to say that passion shouldn't be part of your game plan. It absolutely should be. Your passion is what excites you to contribute your best efforts...motivates you to make the necessary sacrifices...and stimulates you to think up creative and innovative ideas.

I'm simply saying that if you want to become wealthy in a hurry, or even to ensure that you have the best chance to become wealthy at all, you should be passionate about becoming wealthy, *as an end in itself*, as much or even more than you are passionate about the specific field that you make your vehicle to success.

For example, Larry Ellison founded the company that became Oracle in 1977 with $2000 and a passion for a software database he was working on. Today *Forbes* reports that Ellison is worth $18.4 billion.

Naturally, not everyone who sets out to make a success in business will become a billionaire. After all, today there are fewer than 400 billionaires in the entire United States. But the number of millionaires reached 7.5 million individuals or households in 2004. And that number is growing by leaps and bounds. As a matter of fact, from 2003 to 2004 America's pool of millionaires shot up 21%.

If you set your mind on it, I am confident that YOU can be one of them. My point, however, is that your odds of becoming truly wealthy are much better if you aim directly at this target, rather than "hoping" that wealth will "just happen" to you as a result of doing something else.

In this book, we are talking about becoming truly wealthy. My purpose is to show you how to reach the level of financial and career success where you are in control of your own destiny. I want you to soar with the eagles, up there on the level where you can live your dreams–not just live in a nice house, be able to put your kids through college, and take a Hawaiian vacation now and then. To me that isn't being wealthy; it's a nice, upscale, middle-class life (even if you are worth a million "on paper").

In order to achieve success on this level, it is crucial to recognize one thing:

Wealth is a choice.

Wealth happens because an individual chooses it. He decides, "I am absolutely determined to be wealthy," and makes that goal a top priority. Then, fueled by that determination, he takes the concrete steps that are necessary to make it happen.

Focus is the key. You must put aside all competing agendas, overcome all mental reservations, and ignore all distractions. You must say: "I am going to become wealthy" or "I am going to become physically fit" or "I am going to build a wonderful relationship and a happy home"...and you must say: "I will do whatever it takes to create the conditions that I desire" (always within the dictates of conscience and following the conviction of honor).

Subsequent chapters of this book will provide specific guidance in such areas as goal-setting, conditioning your mind for success, selecting a promising market, the meaning of money in our society, and much more. But for now, our subject is your initial *decision* to become wealthy–the primal act of CHOOSING. The power of making this choice, and making it a top priority in your life, cannot be overstated. When you are clear with yourself about your goals and desires, you are reordering your mind, your will, and your life to make those desires a reality.

At age 14, I made the *choice* to become a pilot. I had always dreamed of being one, but that's not the same as choosing to be one. Choosing implies commitments, priorities, and making sacrifices. Choosing implies selecting this option over that, taking this action instead of that, spending my time and effort on this instead of that.

That means if you truly make the *choice* to become wealthy, you will have to keep making that choice over and over again–day after day, week after week, month after month–in a thousand ways, both large and small.

At age 18, I made the choice to become a millionaire. As odd as it may sound, let me say it once again: *being a millionaire is a choice.* If you don't make that choice, deliberately and without any mental reservation, it almost certainly won't happen for you...whether your goal is wealth, fitness, or happiness in relationships.

Why is the power of choice so instrumental in your quest for success? Because each one of us has the ability to do anything, anything at all...just like our junior high school teachers always told us. What holds us back is not the world, but ourselves.

All of us are different in terms of our talents and abilities. But in our power of choosing, all of us are the same. You, me, our neighbors–what makes us different is how we choose to view ourselves and our potential. The fact that we inevitably do make a choice, either consciously or unconsciously–the fact that we cannot help making such a choice–and the fact that our mind ultimately ensures that our choice is acted out in the physical world is what we all share in common.

Therefore, choose consciously. Choose deliberately. And choose wisely.

To truly choose to become wealthy (or healthy, or to achieve any other goal) means choosing to sacrifice certain short-term pleasures and privileges in order to achieve your goal. "To will the end, is to will the means." If you choose to drive to town but refuse to get in the car, refuse to buy gas, and refuse to push down on the accelerator, then your choice is meaningless. In fact, you have not really made a true choice, because again, choice implies commitment and sacrifice.

In the course of building my own company and driving toward my own success, I have frequently given up many things that I really wanted. Often I have wanted to take the night off and go to the movies, but I knew that I had important work to do to build my business. This is a choice that must be made again and again. The seductive and beguiling thought often comes: "Just tonight–just this once, let's make an exception. I won't make it a habit to get away."

But if you keep making these "exceptions," before long you'll discover that your good intentions are "honored more in the breach than the observance." Your intention to build a successful business, or to achieve some other goal that is important to you, has degenerated into empty words and perhaps even self-deception. We simply cannot build a life of success on building blocks of "exceptions." We truly choose a certain long-term outcome, only if our individual, in-the-moment choices consistently support our choice.

Deciding to delay gratification now pays off in terms of achievement and fulfillment later. That future reward is where we must keep our focus. It's important–on a daily basis–that we make it a point to visualize ourselves enjoying that beautiful new home...or reveling in our new attractiveness and energy...or soaring high above the clouds in that aerobatic plane...or basking in the warmth of love and family. Whatever goal we have set for ourselves, if it is truly a product of our deepest dreams and most genuine inspiration, keeping that focus is possible. It's not always easy, but it's possible!

I'm sure we all enjoy having an active social and recreational life. Yet on those occasions when I gave up opportunities for fun and relaxation, I did not view it as making a "sacrifice." Instead, I knew that I was making a free and deliberate decision to do what was really most important to me for my long-term happiness.

Yes, sometimes this meant putting in long hours at the office. As the old joke says, "Launching a new business venture is easy; you only have to work half a day. And the beauty of it is, it doesn't matter which 12 hours of the day you work."

It all comes down to honoring your original commitment to yourself. The only way to achieve success is to set a goal and make it your priority. Notice what I said–YOUR PRIORITY. That doesn't mean "on your priority list;" it means your PRIORITY. Making something your PRIORITY means it comes prior to anything and everything else. It comes *first.* (If it is your top priority, then it often comes second, third, and fourth, too.)

Whenever you put competing activities or desires ahead of your stated goals, then your goals are–more often than not–delayed indefinitely. If your choice is a true one, then you will rise each morning with the same mission in mind, and with the same conviction in your heart–day after day, week after week, month after month, and year after year if necessary.

I believe that all of us are powerful spiritual beings who can, and do, create our own destinies through our power of choice. Choices are our God-given ability. We can choose to be mediocre or we can choose to be awesomely successful. It is a choice that we make on a daily basis, by the things that we tell ourselves subconsciously AND consciously.

Are you ready to CHOOSE to be a *Maverick Millionaire?*

my Maverick 2 Moment

I started taking flying lessons when I was 14. I knew that if you pull back on the yoke you go up; if you push forward, you go down. But I didn't really understand what the flaps did, why airplanes fly (or fall), and what was behind it all.

At age 15 I began ground school. You get a huge stack of manuals, thick books, videotapes, and paperwork. It covers everything from the principles of aerodynamics to airspace regulations. Also map-reading, course plotting, meteorology, instrument functions, engineering, aviation mechanics…

And I thought: how the hell am I ever going to learn all this?

If you just sit and stare at the books, it's easy to let yourself feel overwhelmed. But I cracked open the first book and read the first chapter. I didn't understand it, so I read it again. This time I understood it.

I was only a little bit into the book, but I'd taken that first step. I did the same thing with the second chapter. I did the same thing with the third chapter. And the fourth. And the fifth…

In a relatively short period of time, I knew everything in those books like the back of my hand.

That's where goal-setting comes in. You must impose expectations on yourself and on the situation.

Chapter 5:

A Goal is a Dream With a Deadline

So Start Dreaming...And Buy A Calendar.

Often, when young people learn that I own my own company, they respond: "Oh, that is so cool! I want to start my own business! I want to own my own business someday too!"

"Okay," I say. "What kind of business do you want to own?"

Usually the reply is: "Well, I don't know. I thought maybe I'd do this...or maybe I'd do that...whatever. I just want to own my own business."

Sometimes I follow up by asking: "What do you like doing as far as a career? What are you really good at?" Too often, the answer is: "I don't really know. I haven't discovered it yet. But it will come to me someday!"

People who have this mindset are probably not destined to be business owners. Enthusiasm for the abstract idea of owning your own business is a long, long way from the passion for getting into the trenches and actually doing it. An even more important reason is that successful people know they must take certain intermediate steps between dreams and fulfillment.

The first of these intermediate steps begins with goal-setting.

As author Napoleon Hill famously said, "A goal is a dream with a deadline." Both parts of this definition are equally crucial–the dream, and the deadline. Dreams are where passion begins. If you can't dream it first, it will never become reality. (Even people who win the lottery have to play, and they have to dream of winning in order to play!) To achieve what you want to achieve, you must believe it's possible to do.

Dreaming costs nothing, but it can lead to wonderful realities. This includes literal dreaming, for example when Monster.com CEO Jeff Taylor says the idea for his online job board came to him one night in a dream. Daydreams, too, can be powerful expressions of that all-important inner wealth known as "desire." Napoleon Hill, again, recognized this truth when he said: "Cherish your vision and your dreams as they are the children of your soul; the blueprints of your ultimate achievements."

Not dreaming, on the other hand, can be very expensive. If you settle for doing the same thing day after day, never looking up...never looking ahead...never dreaming of something better...odds are you will achieve the same old results year after year. Worse yet, when the situation changes around you–and it will!–you'll get caught short in yesterday's reality, using yesterday's strategy, and probably getting less than yesterday's results.

To move from dreams to goals, it's necessary to move beyond vague, abstract, non-specific wishes. It's not enough to say "I want to lose weight" or "I want to live in a big house" or "I want to be successful in business." To this you must add specificity. A deadline is part of that specificity, but other details must be added, too. Fill in the picture with numbers, timetables, dollar figures, square footage:

- $ I want to exercise one hour a day, five times a week.
- $ I want to lose 10 pounds.
- $ I want to drive a bright red Ferrari F-430 with tan interior.
- $ I want to live in an 8,000 sq. ft. house in the Spanish Trails development of West Las Vegas.
- $ I want this specific result to happen by 5PM on Oct. 15, 2007, and that other specific result to occur by midnight on May 1, 2009.

Specificity is vital for many reasons. It triggers your conscious and subconscious mind to actually engage with the goal. You solidify the goal in your own mind, and make it much more real, with specifics and a date for achievement. Almost automatically you find yourself thinking: if I'm going to make this intermediate goal by the necessary date, then first I have to do this; it is on the agenda to do.

Specificity also helps ensure that when you arrive at your destination, it's really where you want to be. If you have a big dream in life, then you want to maximize all your efforts in the most efficient way to achieve it. You also shoot as straight as a bullet, and you need a bulls-eye that is the same size as the bullet. If the bulls-eye is the size of Alabama, you can be on target and go a million different directions...most of which may not be satisfying.

Don't feel bad if you don't achieve your goal by your deadline. Use the experience as a learning tool. Set a new goal or a new deadline.

For me, part of the power of goal-setting derives from selecting a goal that is achievable from where I am now–but also one that makes me stretch. Your goals should be just "impossible" enough that it feels like it would be a major achievement when you achieve them…but just "reachable" enough so that you're not too discouraged to actively pursue them.

It's better to risk setting your goals too high than too low. People often don't realize how much they can do, how much power they really have, until they try. I have set goals I did not think I'd be able to meet–then found that not only was I able to meet them, but I exceeded them. Goals can be met and exceeded even if they look outlandish at the time. So the art of goal-setting is walking a fine line between being realistic with yourself, yet also not setting goals so low that you absolutely know that you can easily meet them.

However high you set your goal, attaching a deadline remains a crucial part of the process. Without a date, even if you achieve a goal, it may happen too late. There is a huge difference between getting a bright red Ferrari at age 26 or age 76. I want my Ferrari way before I'm 76. I have a dream, and my dream has a deadline. The specificity of the deadline is a big part of what elevates this vision to a goal so real that I can practically feel the steering wheel in my hands as I write this.

The Power of Putting It on Paper

The next step in translating dreams into goals is: *write it down!*

To understand the power of writing down a goal, you must understand what it means to achieve a goal. It means transferring an idea from inside your head (where it is a dream or a vision) to outside your head (where it acquires weight, color, and texture in the physical world). To make this happen, we need to start with a precise definition of our goal. The more clear, detailed, and vivid our goals become within our own minds, the more power and momentum these goal attain to flow from our imaginations (inside) into our experience (outside).

Writing down your goals can be an almost magical tool to help you begin this process of transferring your dreams from inside to outside.

There are several important reasons why this is so:

- First, the act of writing gives you a chance to interact with your goal in a physical way. This physical experience helps impress the goal more deeply into your subconscious. That's why you should always write your goals out in longhand, rather than typing them on a computer or dictating them into a computer or a tape recorder.

- ¢ Second, once a goal is "realized" on paper, it has taken a HUGE leap. It has moved from the world of imagination, to the world of the five senses. *It now exists in the tangible, physical world.* Now it's a matter of moving it from physical existence on paper to other physical forms: speaking the public words and performing the public actions that will make the goal come to life.
- ¢ Third, a written goal is a private contract with yourself. It means you're not just thinking about it; you're committed to it. Putting a goal on paper, and setting a deadline for achieving that goal, means that we have made our commitment real and inescapable. We have decided. We have made a promise to ourselves. From now on, the goal is part of our life every moment until the goal is realized.
- ¢ Fourth, putting a goal in writing starts the ball rolling for additional action. Sometimes, just the simple act of jotting down a goal in a notebook can stimulate your creativity so much that suddenly, you get all kinds of ideas for the next step to take, and the next and the next...and then an overall strategy may flash into your mind...and more, and more, and more. Why does this happen? Because by writing your goal down, you have sent a clear message to your subconscious: "Hey, we're going to take this idea seriously! Get to work on it right away!"

In addition to writing down your goals, it may also be helpful to illustrate them. You can draw your own sketches, or cut photos out of magazines that symbolize your dream in a concrete way.

I began using this tool on my 21st birthday. That is the day I started what I call my Goal Book. I began by pasting in photos of things that I want: fast cars, boats, a jet plane, great places to visit, great business leaders, speakers addressing audiences. I also cut the word "billionaire" out from a page of *Forbes* Magazine and pasted that in my Goal Book. Yes, one of my goals is to become a billionaire by the time I reach 50!

One thing I wrote in my Goal Book on that 21st birthday was, "I want to fly aerobatics no later than (a certain date) in an Extra 300 airplane." And I cut out a photo of the Extra 300 from a magazine advertisement. Oddly enough, I bought my first real aerobatic airplane, the Extra 300, a short time later. I hadn't reviewed my Goal Book for a while and decided to revisit it once a month. When I opened it, I stopped and my jaw almost dropped because I now owned the Extra 300 that was on that page. Without even consciously thinking, "I am meeting one of my goals," I did. That was one of the most empowering and inspiring moments I ever experienced.

Have you ever heard about people who write themselves checks? Movie stars, famous athletes, and ordinary businessmen and business women often write themselves checks that meet their goals. For example, I know someone who wrote a $100,000 check to himself. He kept it in his wallet for one year. He looked at the check every time he opened his wallet. A year later, not really thinking about the check much after seeing it so often, he opened his wallet to see this "promissory note" that he has written to himself. It was then that he realized that he was now in a position to cash that check...and he did.

I did something similar during my first year as a mortgage lending officer. I put a copy of every single commission check on the mirror over my dresser at home. Every time I went to brush my hair or knot my tie, I was given positive visual reinforcement of my successes. It was encouraging. It reminded me, "You've done it before–you can do it again." By the end of the year, my mirror was covered with so many checks that only a small portion of glass remained free–a little hole for me to see myself, surrounded by money!

These examples are not instances of mysticism or voodoo. They are simply illustrations of the power that wise goal-setting has to help us make our dreams into realities.

A Dream, a Goal, and a Kick in the Pants

After setting our goals, the next step is to create a plan. A goal says where you want to go and when you want to arrive...a plan is the roadmap for how you'll get there.

On the night of my 21st birthday, I established another major goal in my life. As with most goals, it began with a dream. I was sharing a beer with Tom, one of my mentors who had also become a good friend. At the time, I was still working as a mortgage lending officer in a large, established company.

Although it was my birthday and I was supposed to be celebrating, the truth is I was crying in my beer. "My account rep is leaving," I told Tom. "She's expecting a baby and she wants to become a fulltime mother. And when she's gone, my beautiful network of realtors is going to go with her. What the hell am I going to do?"

"What do you *want* to do?" Tom asked.

I confessed my secret desire to open my own company. Remember, I had dreamed of owning my own company and being active in real estate since I was just a kid.

"What kind of company do you want to open?" Tom said.

I took a deep breath and said I wanted to focus on the unconventional, high-margin, private money business.

"Well, why don't you?" Tom said in a reasonable, friendly tone of voice. "You've been a private money investor for almost three years now, you know enough to do it."

"I don't have a big enough network of private investors," I said. "I'm not even sure there are enough private investors out there to make it work."

"BULL!" Tom said. "Las Vegas is booming. This town is positively choking on millionaires who don't know what to do with all their liquid assets. The private money lending company idea sounds like a winner to me. In fact, Jordan, if you don't do it, I will."

"What?" I choked.

"You've got 15 days to put a business plan on my desk," Tom said. "And if you don't, I'll go out and do your idea myself."

"WHAT!!??"

"If you don't follow through, which you probably won't, then I will open my own private money lending business. I will do a better job of it than you ever could, anyway. In fact, you probably *can't* do it, period. You're all talk and no action."

I sputtered and fumed and said, *Oh, yes I would* have that business plan on his desk in two weeks–and damn, what kind of friend was he, stealing my idea!?

Tom was a great friend, of course. His challenge was exactly the kick in the pants that I needed to get me moving. That night, I wrote in my Goal Book that I would start my own business by a certain date in the not-too-distant future, and that I would become a multimillionaire soon after. These were ambitious goals, and at some level I thought they might be unattainable. But part of me also believed that maybe...just maybe...I could do it.

Two weeks later, I proudly placed a finished business plan on Tom's desk. That month, I applied for my mortgage broker's license. There was no state license test, but I did have to pass a background check; and I had to prove that I met certain minimum requirements for net worth. In May of 2004, with my mortgage broker's license in hand, I resigned from the mortgage lending company where I worked, and opened my company, a private money lending firm with one employee: Jordan Wirsz.

Several months later, I realized my goal of becoming a multimillionaire.

My present goal is to increase my net worth. That is what I have written down in my Goal Book at the moment. I want to retire by age 50, and as mentioned, my goal is to be a billionaire by the time I retire. There is one hell of a long way to go to accomplish that, but I know it definitely can be done. (If I met it at 55, I'd still be very happy!)

Taking Your First Step

The next couple of pages include a 20-minute exercise that I want you to do before reading the next chapter. It is, of course, an exercise in goal-setting. To some, it may seem a bit silly to go through this exercise. But I assure you it's a very serious dialog with the *one person* who can make your dreams come true: yourself.

If you simply cannot make yourself go through such an exercise, I would respectfully suggest that maybe you need to look at whether you're harboring some deep-seated (even unconscious) beliefs that your life is hopeless and that there's no point in actually *doing* anything concrete to achieve your goals. If so, then before anything else, you need to focus on accountability–because it is you, not your parents or your circumstances or your bank balance, that determine your fate.

If you do complete the exercise on the following pages, congratulations. You have taken your first concrete, physical, and spiritual steps toward making your dreams a reality!

A Crucial Exercise in Goal-Setting

First, go to a quiet room with no one else around. Turn the lights to a medium intensity, where it is bright enough to read, but not blinding. Make sure you are free from distraction. Turn off your phone; turn off the TV and any music, unless it is calm, slow classical or jazz music.

I want you to get out a large piece of blank paper. Now, I want you to take two minutes and write down your most important five goals. Make sure they are evenly spaced on the entire sheet of paper. These goals can be physical things you wish to have, or a lifestyle you wish to live. These goals can be anything you wish them to be.

Look at each goal individually, and then look at them collectively. Ask yourself if these goals are really that important to you, and if they are, what you are willing to do to achieve them. Ask yourself if these five goals fit together, or if it is unlikely to have all five goals mesh together. Ponder these goals for 60 seconds each.

Now, look at your first goal. Ask yourself to be specific. Next to this goal, write down as many specifics as you can about it. For example:

1. *I want to own a luxury car one day.*
   Specifics: It will be a Ferrari 430 Modena, bright fire-engine red. It will be a brand-new model, with chrome wheels, and black tinted windows. It will have tan leather interior, with my initials inscribed in the headrest.
2. *I will live in a big house.*
   Specifics: I will live in Pacific Palisades on the California Beach. My house will be in a gated community. It will have a six-car garage, no less than 7,500 square feet of living space, and a spectacular view of the ocean from the backyard and master suite. The house will be tan colored with a palm tropical theme, and the entire west side of the home will be covered with windows overlooking the ocean. My house will be two stories tall, featuring a wine cellar, theater room, and large entertaining area combined with the kitchen, overlooking my 80 foot by 70 foot swimming pool, with water falls and a Jacuzzi, surrounded by green grass and small coy fish ponds.

Now, take 120 seconds (two minutes) with each goal once more. Look at the specifics that you wrote. Ask yourself if that is all you can think of. Now enjoy the image, closing your eyes if you wish, dreaming the soon to be reality of your goals. Savor the taste of these images in your mind...

Now look once more at these goals. Next to each of these goals, you will have 90 seconds to write down the *course of action* you plan on taking to achieve these goals. Write as many details as you can. Be specific of how you are going to make these goals happen. What sources and what routes are you going to take in order to succeed? If you find yourself not being specific, and being vague, force yourself to be specific about how you are going to plan your success.

After you have completed the exercise, look back at your goals, specifics, and plan of actions. Ask yourself if that is the route you really want to go, or if it is the only route you know how to go. Remember the reasons you strive for these goals, and why they are so very important to you. Now fold that piece of paper, and view it once a day, thinking about its importance, until you have achieved that goal.

Now I have another exercise for you to try. This will help you mesh your subconscious and your conscious thoughts into what you want them to be.

Going back to the five goals you wrote down from the exercise above, ask yourself if those are goals that your subconscious does believe you can achieve. If they are, great! If not, get five goals that your subconscious doesn't agree that you can accomplish. If you question whether your goals are suitable for this exercise, just ask yourself if there is a voice deep inside you that says, "you can't, it's just an unrealistic dream."

Now take those five goals, and ask yourself what your subconscious is arguing with your conscious mind about. Take those goals, and turn them into five affirmations you can say to yourself, with specifics. For example:

1. *I want a bright red Ferrari F-430.*
   Affirmation: I will own a Ferrari F-430 by year-end 2006.
2. *I want to live in a beautiful home in Pacific Palisades.*
   Affirmation: I will own a home in Pacific Palisades by year 2010 because I want and deserve it.

Now take the five goals that you chose, and each morning, before you start your day, go to your bathroom mirror, and say those five affirmations. You must do this for 30 days straight without interruption. If you miss a day, your 30 day calendar begins all over again.

At the end of the 30 days, you will notice a dramatic change in your attitude. You will begin to approach the questions of your life with a positive attitude of "I can–and I will, because I can." Your dreams of owning a Ferrari or a large house in the Palisades won't seem so unrealistic. You will also begin to form ideas and plans for how to achieve those goals. Most importantly, you will begin to believe, within yourself, that you CAN achieve them and that you DESERVE them.

It is my strong recommendation that each and every day of your life, for the rest of your life, you should continue this exercise. You will begin to come up with new ideas for goals, and new ideas for routes to take in order to realize them. In addition, continuing this exercise will also keep your mind focused and believing. Too often, people will stop performing these mind-setting and life changing psychological exercises, to find themselves slipping back into their old habits and "I can't" attitudes.

To continue positive results, you must continue affirming within your conscious and subconscious mind that YOU CAN, YOU WILL, YOU DESERVE, and YOU BELIEVE!

Chapter 6:

A Call to Action

There Is No Substitute for Action.

At a seminar I attended once, General Electric CEO Jack Welch quoted a life-changing line from the Reverend Dr. Vance Havner. When I say "life-changing," I mean that literally. I think about Havner's idea literally every day. It is one of the most powerful ideas I've ever heard.

Welch said: *"It's not enough to stare up the steps; we must step up the stairs."*

This is a call to action. This is where we truly begin to separate the men from the boys, the women from the girls, and the successes from the failures. It's great to have a dream, and it's even better to have a specific goal. It's better yet to have a plan of attack to achieve that goal.

But all of these are worth nothing, unless we follow them up with ACTION. And we must start at the bottom, on the first step of the stairway to success!

> **MAVERICK MOTIVATOR:**
>
> You can be wealthy, just watch your debt! According to the Pew Research Center, the biggest goals for Generation Y are wealth and fame, but their greatest challenges are money, finances, and debt.

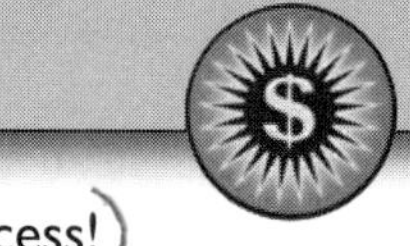

Too many people conceive a goal, and then…they just sit there. They look up at this ultimate goal; they gape at this seemingly infinite stairway between themselves and their dream, and forget that they must start climbing the stairway with one step, then another, and another. These people look at the path, but they don't take the first step down the path. Instead they scratch their heads, rub their chins, and say: Gee, that's a long path. Or: Wow, I really want to get to the top of this stairway. *But nothing seems to make them take that first step.*

The people who succeed in life are those who are predisposed to ACTION. They see that first step and they start stepping. They don't always know where they're going, but they keep stepping! As soon as they see the goal, almost immediately their next question is: "What do I do to take the first steps, and what are the repercussions of going from Point A to Point B? What are the next steps that I will have to take or want to take, after I arrive at my destination?"

People who delay taking that first step often say, "I am waiting for inspiration." Somehow, for most people that inspiration never comes. By definition, they are looking for inspiration because they don't have it. They don't have the burning desire that would prompt them to act, to commit themselves, to learn, to work, to sacrifice.

To those people who say, "I am waiting for inspiration," my reply is very simple. You don't really want to achieve your stated goal–because if you did, you'd already have inspiration, and it would take you down the path; then you would achieve your goal. You don't want it badly enough.

Motivation versus Inspiration: Empty Calories versus Nutrition

It's important to understand the difference between motivation and inspiration.

- Motivation comes from *without,* and it's usually a *short-term* phenomenon...as when a football coach gives a rousing halftime pep talk, or a motivational speaker gets an audience all worked up.
- Inspiration comes from *within,* and for that reason, it's a *permanent* fountain of joy and desire bubbling up from our own hearts. True inspiration never runs dry; it rarely needs to be replenished. Instead, inspiration replenishes us.

I have spent my life trying to understand my own psychology and what makes people successful. And I have come to the conclusion that waiting for inspiration is a complete waste of time. People are not hit with "sudden bursts of inspiration." They are hit with sudden bursts of motivation–external stimuli–but inspiration is either constant, or it's non-existent.

Motivation can be exciting, but it lacks long-term value, which means it can actually be dangerous to your financial health. I learned this lesson the hard way. At the age of 13, I was sucked into what I *believed* to be groups of successful people–the "multi-level marketers." As a youngster, I wasted thousands of dollars in multi-level marketing companies.

While it's possible to make money in multi-level marketing, I'm not a fan or these organizations. Oh, yes, I have met some people who became very successful in MLMs. In fact, some MLM winners make much more money than I do at present time. (At least, they say they do.)

At the same time, no one can deny the fact that most people who get involved in multi-level marketing companies as entry level "representatives" or "marketing managers" do NOT make it big. In fact, statistics show that most of them fail. But, if MLMs offer such a dismal success rate, why do they continue to exist, and even flourish? Why do people continue flocking to them?

The reason for the seeming success of most MLMs is that they are not really selling the product or service that they claim to market. They are actually selling "a smile and a shoeshine"...the excitement and illusion of short-term motivation. In my experience, most MLMs are built on the worst kind of motivational speakers, the kind who populate their rallies by offering hollow hopes and empty promises.

Many people (especially those who have had little or no monetary success) tend to subconsciously believe that they can become rich in one day from one of these programs. Why? Because they get to talk to a very wealthy person who made lots of money from the MLM program. Maybe they feel, during their contacts with such a person, wealth will somehow "rub off."

Well, it's true that the company you keep has a profound influence on your life and on your chances for success (see Chapter 9 on mentors). But just rubbing shoulders with a successful MLM executive now and then—just listening in on a twice-weekly conference call with other entry-level reps like yourself–is not enough, by itself, to move you from poverty to wealth.

Too many people who join MLMs at the bottom level spend so much time getting "pumped up" and "excited" about the *idea* of making money that they forget to work at actually getting the business and really *making* money. Those who do attempt to make the MLM program work, too often find themselves spending hours, days, or weeks trying to get family members, friends, and co-workers to subscribe to the company's get-rich-quick scheme.

Finally, most of those who DO make millions from MLMs earn those millions by cycling vast numbers of people through the strainer bowl of human desire. Basically, MLM's exploit their own people rather than providing a genuine product or service.

Don't get me wrong; motivational speakers have their place. The reputable ones, the Zig Ziglars and Tony Robbins, don't sell surface; they sell substance. They may create a certain aura of glamour, but they don't promise "the way" to become wealthy. In most cases, the people who buy their books and tapes and attend their seminars are *already* doing well in their careers. They are merely seeking to take themselves to the next level. They aren't looking for get-rich-quick schemes, but for solid guidance about the habits and thought patterns that lead to enhanced success.

Start Small.
Start the Ball Rolling.
But Whatever You Do, START!

Mistaking motivation for inspiration is only one of the obstacles that prevents people from taking action. Another block that prevents action is perfectionism, and it is deadly. Too many people assume, consciously or otherwise, that they cannot afford to make a single mistake. They feel it's better to do nothing than to try some action that may turn out to be less than perfect.

Nothing could be further from the truth. As G.K. Chesterton once joked, "Anything worth doing is worth doing badly." There is more than a grain of wisdom in this joke. The fact is, jumping in and doing *something* is almost always better than sitting around doing *nothing*. Action, even an unsuccessful action, at least has the virtue of getting us started. Better yet, once we act, we leave the airy realm of theory and enter into the solid realm of experience. In this bracing encounter with reality, we may get bruised now and then–but something wonderful almost always happens, too: we LEARN.

Dave Thomas (founder and CEO of the Wendy's hamburger chain) and his partner Phil Clauss are textbook examples of how even a rocky start can teach you how to succeed in a big way. Way back in the early 1950s, decades before the idea of Wendy's was born, Thomas and Clauss were in the restaurant business together, running a single store. At a restaurant convention, Clauss met an old, white-bearded fellow named "Colonel" Harland Sanders. The Colonel had a special recipe for a product he called Kentucky Fried Chicken…

Trouble was, Colonel Sanders didn't know a darned thing about production or marketing. When Dave Thomas and Phil Clauss met him, the Colonel was literally selling KFC out of his car (a white Cadillac that matched his white suit, white goatee, and white mustache).

Fortunately, 18-year-old Dave Thomas knew plenty about food production and creative use of resources from having served as a mess sergeant in the Army. (In fact, Thomas said the Armed Forces are one of the best places to learn entrepreneurship.) Equally fortunate was the fact that Phil Clauss, the restaurant owner, knew a few crude basics of promotion. Together, Thomas and Clauss decided to take on KFC as a franchise commodity.

Their first step was to offer Kentucky Fried Chicken as take-out in specially designed red and white cardboard buckets with the Colonel's picture on the outside. What a concept! This small step made KFC a huge success, even though the original buckets were a disaster. The wax paraffin coating melted all over the food, the customer's clothes, and the seats of their cars.

Thomas and Clauss didn't let that setback stop them for one minute. They found a manufacturer who could create a better lining for the inside of their bucket. They also improved the Colonel's portrait and logo on the outside. The success of the product led to their next step: the decision to build a national brand around the Colonel's image and folksy personality. Then came a revolution in fast food: TV marketing, a countrywide chain of dedicated KFC restaurants, and eventually, a worldwide empire.

Small Steps Can Lead to BIG Results

A third block that prevents some people from taking action is the belief that they must make big, bold, dramatic steps from Day One. Like the fear of making a mistake, this belief in "all or nothing" is a debilitating delusion. As the Chinese say, the journey of a thousand miles begins with a single step. Life teaches us that the smallest action is related, in a direct chain of cause-and-effect, to the largest outcome.

One person who knows the truth of this lesson is Captain James Pulliam, the U.S.Army's 2004 specialist medical corpsman of the year. By professional training Capt. Pulliam is a dietician, but he has also served as a company commander in peacetime, has taken combat paratrooper training, and has served our nation in wartime Iraq. Sometimes, said Capt. Pulliam, whether in peace or war, in administration or in combat, we run into a situation that is unprecedented. But whatever problems arise, he said, it's vital to decide and act quickly, based on available information. Not only should we risk making mistakes, he says, we should also be humble enough to start small and let our efforts grow organically.

"In most cases, we don't have time to wait until we know everything there is to know about a situation," says Capt. Pulliam. "We don't have time to agonize over crafting the 'perfect' plan. As Patton always said, a good plan today is better than a perfect plan tomorrow. There is a power in taking action, on whatever scale you start. But do it NOW."

One example of the power of taking action, even small actions, was seen at an Army base in Colorado Springs. Capt. Pulliam and his supervisor Colonel Kostner launched a civilian wellness program for Department of Defense employees on the base. Salaried and professional civilian employees were given time off to exercise three or four hours each week as part of their job. "When we originally announced it," the captain recalled, "we thought we'd have overwhelming numbers of applicants–hundreds and hundreds of people. Where would we put all of them?"

To their surprise, at first fewer than 50 civilians on the entire post took up the offer. Capt. Pulliam admitted that he and the colonel were disappointed. But then, he says, a funny thing happened. "Once that program got rolling, it made a disproportionate impact," Pulliam explains. "To begin with, we saw big benefits to those who did participate. At least 10 lost significant weight and improved their lab values. The first 50 are setting a good example for their colleagues. The word is spreading. And now the program is really growing." He has seen similar programs start with just one squad, then spread to an entire company, and finally to an entire base.

In the mind of Capt. Pulliam, the lesson of such efforts is very simple. "We must have the vision to take the first step, AND we must have the patience to let things grow, to let them take their natural course," he says. "That is not the American way. In this country we are impatient. We want instant results: this year, this quarter, this week, NOW. And if we don't get those instant results, then we very quickly denounce the program as a failure and move on to something else. The truth is, that is not how things work. Change doesn't happen overnight, but it can be done."

Humble Beginnings Can Lead to Grand Endings

One more typical mistake that people allow to block them from action is the notion that it's only worthwhile to "start at the top." This notion takes any number of forms:

- ¢ If we can't rent an office in swankiest part of town, with the latest computers and state-of-the-art communications, then let's not bother to open our doors.
- ¢ If we can't run on the best track in the city, with the latest $300 running shoes and designer track suit, then let's not bother to start a jogging program.
- ¢ If we can't begin our career with a big salary and a corner office with a view, we won't accept a position in that industry.

This "start at the top" mentality is not only egotistical, it's an unsound business practice as well. You don't build a house from the roof down; you build it from the foundation up! Starting small, cheap, and humble gives you a chance to learn your business, a chance to grow your company organically, and a chance to expand your position in synch with your growing professionalism and rising revenues.

Did you know that Michael Eisner started in the mailroom at the Walt Disney Corporation? Eventually, he rose to command a worldwide, multimedia, entertainment and communications empire.

I launched my company from my living room, if you want to get right down to it. When the company "officially" opened for business, I took space in an Executive Suites facility. Basically that means you rent a desk and a phone, while sharing a secretary with a lot of other small-timers.

It was not until we had been in business for a full year, and had established a solid clientele and a VERY substantial monthly cash flow, that my company purchased its own prestigious suite of offices.

It's not where you begin but where you end up that counts.

When we take that first, small, modest, imperfect step, we probably won't be able to foresee the ultimate long-term results. Beginnings, then, are a time for faith. We simply have to trust that the results are there, over the horizon, waiting for us. I believe that if a dream or burning desire is planted deep within our hearts, somehow a way will be made for that dream to be realized, and for that desire to be fulfilled. Faith is one more of those magnificent inner resources that makes us "rich inside" and can help make us "rich outside."

If you want to achieve wealth, happiness, and success, there is only one way to do it. Have faith...take that first, small, imperfect step.

Chapter 7:

Money is the Fruit of Hard Work

America has a strange, love-hate relationship with wealth. On the one hand, the wealthy are admired, emulated, and even fawned over. Material goods and wealth are envied, coveted, desired, and often taken as the confirmation of a person's ultimate worth. In our country, the ultimate yardstick for pragmatic success (or the ultimate test for people who are suspected of being "all hat and no cattle") is: "If you're so smart, why aren't you rich?"

On the other hand, the wealthy are resented, reviled, and even hated. Many people assume that if you wear a Rolex or drive a Ferrari, you're arrogant, pretentious, and egotistical. There is a widespread belief that money–or the inordinate love of money–is the root of all evil; that material wealth is somehow un-spiritual; that poverty is the mark of virtue; and that as Jesus said, "You cannot serve both God and Mammon."

In a variation on this view, we often get the mixed message that it's great to *have* money, but somehow it's wrong to be overly concerned about *getting* money. It's acceptable (barely) to want to be financially successful, but only if you don't want it "too much." And it's okay to work like a dog to get ahead, but it's wrong to want the material rewards of your work, which are derided as "luxuries."

Put it all together and you have the great American double-bind:

Money is good. Ambition and desire are good. Wealth is good.	Money is evil. Ambition and desire is evil. Wealth is evil.

If you have absorbed these messages in whole or in part–even subconsciously–then you may be conflicted in your deepest attitudes toward wealth, material gain, and success.

Since you are reading this book, I assume that at least part of your conscious self is interested in achieving success, maybe even in attaining outrageous wealth. At the same time, somewhere in the back of your head, a little voice may be warning: *"You shouldn't care so much about crass material values. You should be focused on something higher, nobler, and better than mere money."* Or you may hear a faint voice that suggests: *"It's okay to hope for wealth, but it's not okay to actually do anything to make it happen."*

Take Charge of Your Beliefs, or They'll Take Charge of You

If we don't resolve these conflicted attitudes about money, wealth, and material success in our own minds once and for all, then we are carrying an unnecessary burden–perhaps even an insurmountable barrier–in our quest for success. Before you can maximize your efforts to attain success, especially monetary success, you must get clear in your own mind about the **meaning of wealth** and your own **worthiness to be wealthy.**

Otherwise, no matter how hard you work…no matter how brilliantly you plan…you will unconsciously sabotage yourself. One way or another, your subconscious mind will arrange events to ensure that you won't get wealthy…or that if you do attain wealth, you won't keep it…or that if you keep it, you won't enjoy it.

As for the strange notion that being poor is a mark of virtue, take it from someone who's lived it: there is absolutely nothing noble or ennobling about poverty. Quite to the contrary, in fact. No less a moral authority than Mahatma Gandhi declared that "Poverty is a form of violence," and I believe that statement with all my heart.

So if money is *not* the root of all evil…and if money is *not* an automatic sign of virtue, either…then exactly what is it?

Money is a neutral commodity, as good or bad as the person who uses it.

- $ If a person has a selfish, corrupt streak, then money will give him the chance to indulge those negative tendencies.
- $ If a person has a generous, loving heart and a vigorous social conscience, then money will afford her the opportunity to express those positive qualities, too.

Later in this chapter, I will consider wealth from a social or political point of view. But for now, I just want to share my personal experiences with attitudes toward money, and with the relationship of money to morality.

> I grew up in a household where (a) we didn't have any money; but (b) there was absolutely nothing wrong with *wanting* all the money you could get. My parents saw no moral conflict between godliness and wealth. Neither do I.

Given these mental and spiritual values, our family's often-precarious finances only served to sharpen my hunger to become wealthy. No wonder I decided at age five that I wanted to be a multimillionaire someday! Since the Wirsz family never seemed to have much money around, at an early age I set out to earn my own money.

I began my first business at age 13. Flash forward 10 years to today, when I am the CEO of a fast-growing, thriving financial enterprise. From the seasoned perspective of a battle-scarred, 24 year old business veteran, I can speak from personal experience. Far from corrupting my morals, money has given me a chance to strengthen certain parts of my character–particularly my spirituality.

At the risk of sounding immodest, I would like to share a story that is deeply meaningful to me. The church I belong to supports an orphanage down in La Mission, Mexico. It's an impoverished community in a desert valley, and our congregation provides year-round donations to cover the orphans' food, laundry costs, salaries for care providers, the works.

"Mission: Possible" In A Small Town In Mexico

Every six months, our church selects a needy family in La Mission, Mexico and builds a home for them. During these visits, congregation members are permitted to pitch tents in an orphanage's compound, use the institution's public showers and toilets, and use the orphanage's small warehouse to hold meetings, prepare meals, and store our materials.

A couple of summers ago, I was fortunate to have the opportunity to join one of these projects. We drove down to La Mission to build a home for a single-parent family whose mother had run off and abandoned them. The father was raising his seven kids alone. They lived in a horrible shack made out of mismatched pieces of plywood. Tin roof, dirt floors, no running water, no electricity. The shack was divided into two "rooms" by a hanging sheet.

By the time our group arrived, the foundation had already been poured. We rolled up our sleeves and went to work. Our team built a frame, installed the siding, put on the roof, and installed a stove, wiring, and lights. There was no heating or air conditioning, but in three days flat we built a decent home for that family to live in. It was one of the most joyful and rewarding experiences of my life.

There is a direct connection between building that house in La Mission, Mexico, and building my own nest egg in Las Vegas, Nevada. Money gave me not just the *means* to contribute; it actually helped spark and heighten my *desire* to do so. Once I began to experience financial success, I began to feel a strong sense of gratitude to my Higher Power, and a growing eagerness to give back some of the blessings that I have received.

(And it doesn't stop here. I intend to keep giving as long as I live, and I know that whatever I give will come back to me tenfold in spiritual rewards and in personal happiness. For me, the prospect of having a positive influence on the lives of others on an ever-widening scale, makes everything else that I do seem all the more worthwhile. At any rate, I'm certainly going to do everything I can to achieve this goal–just as I do with all my other goals.)

The Amazing Power Of Money... When Wielded ByThe Most Generous People On Earth

The world's largest charitable foundation, endowed by Microsoft Chairman Bill Gates and his wife Melinda, gives away billions of dollars to a variety of causes such as college scholarships to minorities, AIDS prevention, and efforts to control diseases that strike mainly in the Third World. The Gates' philanthropic foundation also provides 90% of the current world budget for the campaign to eliminate polio.

Tens of thousands of similarly admirable examples of philanthropy could also be cited. These range from huge enterprises run the by the world's rich and famous–the Ford Foundation, the Eli Lilly Endowment Group, and the like–to the dozens of private individuals who I know personally–to the millions of anonymous Americans who make generous donations to charities and other worthy social causes. In addition, let's not forget the record-setting level of contributions to the International Red Cross, the American Red Cross, the United Way, and countless others following the Asian tsunami of December 2004, and the Hurricane Katrina disaster of 2005.

(Money, the root of all evil? Nonsense! With the issue of financial security off the table, you are free to devote your personal time to the quest for a better and nobler quality of life. Money is liberating. Money opens the door to self-fulfillment. Money gives us the leeway for inner development. Money empowers us to help our fellow man and woman.

If we lack resources such as time and money to give, how can we practice charity? We can't. And in today's fast-moving, electronic-transaction, liquid-asset world, the resource that moves the fastest and does the most good is MONEY.

And that's not all…

**It's YOUR Money –
Because It Represents
YOUR Sweat, Creativity, and Courage**

I don't want to appear to suggest that the only good of wealth lies in our ability to give it away.

In a free-market economy, where every man and woman earns his or her own keep, our money is just that: ours. We earned it through our own efforts. We created it through our innovation. We deserve it! Therefore, we have every right to keep our money and to use it in whatever way we see fit…whatever way gives us the most joy and satisfaction.

Money is the just reward for a job well done.

Money is a way of storing up the fruits of our labor, just as a battery is a way of storing up electricity. Money is a set of wings that we build for ourselves, through our own blood, sweat, and sacrifice. Who is to say that after building those wings, we have no right to spread our wings and fly?

In this sense, money is the most moral commodity that you can imagine. Money gives us the amplitude to express our personalities fully and joyously.

Did you ever stop to think about the fact that, at least in the United States, money also has a constructive *political* meaning? In this country, money is the symbol of a free exchange of values between people who are equals under the law.

In America, we like to say: *"My money is as good as anybody else's."*

The power that we assign to money in a free-enterprise system is an expression of the fact that freedom and equality are the ultimate ruling principles of our society. Not government force, not personal "connections," and not religious orthodoxy. In our system, the very existence of money presupposes and symbolizes the right to own private property, the right to associate and trade voluntarily with others, the right to be treated equally, and the right to be free.

Finally, as philosopher Ayn Rand often said, "Wealth is the product of man's capacity to think."

As a refugee from Communist Russia, Ms. Rand admired one thing above all else about her adopted country. She loved the fact that Americans instinctively understand our economic "pie" is not of fixed size; it can be grown. In fact, it can be *expanded without limits.*

Americans, said Ms. Rand, instinctively "get it" that the size of our economic pie results directly from our brains, creativity, courage, and willingness to work. Therefore, we don't have to waste our lives in unproductive fights over "who gets the biggest slice." We can simply keep growing the pie. The only limits are the constraints of our imagination and our will. In other words, ultimately there are no limits at all. There is plenty for everyone...and tomorrow, there will be even more.

Let each person claim that share of America's ever-growing national wealth, which they *earn*–through their own efforts!

Never, ever be ashamed of your desires to earn money, to possess money, or to spend money!

Chapter 8:

The School of Hard Knocks

If somebody came to me and said, "I want to start my own business. I have a little capital—under $100,000—and I have a great business plan. What's your advice?" My first instinct would be to say: Make sure you know what you're getting into and that it is what you really want to do.

And yet the plain fact is, a beginning business owner doesn't have a clue what it takes to make a successful company. I didn't have a clue when I started; nobody in this world has a clue before they start. You simply have to get into it and start to learn by doing. It's called "The School of Hard Knocks."

It used to bother me when people would say, "You've got to pay your dues." I used to think, "Damn it, I don't want to pay dues–I want a short-cut to success!" But the School of Hard Knocks is not necessarily about dues-paying or putting in your time, just so you can say you've got X years of experience. To me, entering this school means "learning by doing." Regardless of whether you're an entrepreneur, an artist, an athlete, or an inventor–there is nothing so valuable to any ambitious person as learning what NOT to do, from experience.

It may sound strange, but nine out of ten successful CEOs in this country would say their success has not been from learning what to do right, but learning what mistakes to avoid, what traps to evade, and what illusions to see through. This is not only the case with famous executives running billion-dollar businesses; in fact, this idea is especially important for young people who are just starting in their careers.

"It's easier to screw things up at this point than to keep growing," said Mike Domek, who founded TicketsNow.com, the world's largest online marketplace for secondary event tickets. Domek began his company in his early 30s with $100 and a two-line phone in a one-bedroom apartment. Five years later, before he hit 40 years old, he had a staff of 110 people and annual revenues of $40 million.

When Domek talked about how easy it is to screw things up when a company is young, he was talking about the value of the School of Hard

Knocks: learning what NOT to do. Domek's education in that school came during the seven years *before* he founded TicketsNow. That's when he learned the ropes with his earlier start-up company in a similar market.

If you're smart, you never graduate from the School of Hard Knocks. You commit yourself to a lifelong learning process of trying new things, seeing what happens, and then refining your approach to make it work the next time (if the first try failed), or to make it work better (if the first try succeeded).

In my own field, the lending and real estate business, I constantly find people want to break in with a sort of "insurance policy" by reading books about it or talking to people about it. Beginner's constantly ask: "I want to get into the real estate business; are there any books that can guarantee results? Are there any courses I can take, that will teach me how to be a sure-fire success?"

The short answer is no. There is not any single manual for you to read, and not a single course you can take, that will all of a sudden make you magically successful. Reading this book won't make you magically or instantly successful, either. I can't make you happy or "rich inside" and "rich outside"...but I can show you how you can make YOURSELF successful by capitalizing on your resources.

Again, this principle of being a perpetual student applies to any field. For example, take aviation, my first passion. Experienced pilots tell beginners: "The day you stop learning is the day you die."

Oh, yes there are second chapters in American lives!

Whoever said, "There are no second chapters in American lives," obviously wasn't paying attention. This country is preeminently the place for lives to have second chapters, third chapters, fourth chapters, and beyond!

Two of the finest perpetual students (I can't say graduates) of the School of Hard Knocks were Henry Ford and Thomas Edison. They also happened to be two of the great geniuses of American industry and science, and they additionally happened to be friends. Both men had very useful things to say about the philosophy of their favorite "school."

Ford said: "Failure is just the chance to begin again, more intelligently." He was right, of course. If you check out the stories of most successful entrepreneurs, you'll find most went through booms and bankruptcies–often several times—before finally achieving steady success.

As for Thomas Edison, when he was trying to invent the electric light, he tried hundreds and hundreds of materials for the bulb's filament–the wire that would carry the electric current and throw off the illumination. Finally he reached 1,000 attempts without discovering the material he wanted. One of his assistants asked him if he felt discouraged by so many failures. Edison replied: "I have not failed. I've just found 1,000 ways that won't work." He explained that every attempt had yielded a positive result, because it taught him something definite.

> **MAVERICK MOTIVATOR:**
> No college, no problem! The majority of young people are not enrolled in college. In fact only 25-35% of 18-35 year olds are in college.

Personally, I would go even farther than Ford, who said failure is an opportunity, and I would go father than Edison, who said for him failure did not exist. In my opinion, *failure is necessary.* You cannot be successful without failure.

Let me explain what I mean by that. Nobody in this world wakes up and says: this is how I will achieve my goals and without question, it's going to work. There is nobody alive who has a 100% success rate. In fact, most people have much less than a 50% success rate–whether it's in baseball, business, or ballet. That's why, although I'm not enthusiastic about some college educations, I love the concept of one class at Harvard Business School called "Failure 101." In this class, students are expected to start three projects during the course, and to have three failures. That's right; they plan to fail. But they are also expected to *learn important lessons* from every one of those failures, lessons that carry the seeds of future success. Just like real life!

Here is the big secret of the School of Hard Knocks: even if you succeed less than 50% of the time, your successes can still outweigh your failures! When you have an occasional success, it provides the capital, the encouragement, and the energy to keep going...keep learning...and keep trying. (Maybe that's why Winston Churchill said his personal definition of success was "the ability to go from one failure to another, without loss of enthusiasm.")

My own introduction to the School of Hard Knocks began with the multi-level marketing company that I wrote about in the previous chapter. I tried selling the MLM's herbal supplements. Financially, it was a failure–but in terms of my business education, it was a major success.

> - This experience taught me the difference between motivation and inspiration.
> - It taught me that success cannot be handed to you on a platter as a paint-by-numbers, formulaic program.
> - It taught me to put my faith in myself, not in some big organization with an impressive façade.

In my own business and life, I have failed many times. But often, a failure can lead to a success later on. At age 14 I tried to buy a helicopter kit online but found I didn't have enough money. However, the owner said if I helped him sell the item, which he was having trouble doing, he would pay me a $2,500 commission. My mother signed the contract for me since I was a minor. The owner sent me some product specs and sales materials, and said: "Have at it, kid." I went back on the Internet and found every website on the planet that offered free classified advertising. In early 1996, just after my 15th birthday, I found a buyer for the helicopter kit and earned my first commission as an aircraft broker/salesman.

Learn To Handle "Failure"
the Way A Child Learns to Walk
(Fall Down, Get Up, Let Go, Move On)

The way to handle failures is by taking them in stride. Failure is not the worst thing in the world. You say, "Damn! Well, I'm not going to do that again next time." And you move on.

Too many people have a tendency to focus on failures and not let it go. This is true in business and it's true in personal relationships. I have seen people who can't work, can't concentrate, and can't do anything right, because they're obsessed over a relationship failure or a career failure that happened two, three, or more years ago. Such people hang onto feeling bad about their failures much longer than they hang onto feeling good about their successes. And that needs to be consciously changed.

Think about it. If every infant who was learning to walk held it against themselves each time they fell down, no one would ever learn to walk!

Children that age are too young for self-condemnation; they just get up and try again. This is not unusual; it's the most natural thing in the world–until it's trained out of us. We're all born with the right instinct, with optimistic attitudes, with the fundamental expectation of success. We have an inborn tendency to do whatever it takes to make things happen, and to keep trying until we get our way. The child who falls down and tries again has adults encouraging her: try it again! Or, a kid learning to ride a bicycle is another great example. Dads and moms don't say, "Sorry, Junior, you didn't learn how to ride the bike the first time, so give up and we'll sell your bike." They say, "Try it again…one more time." It's positive affirmation that turns failure into success.

In this sense, successful people remain childlike all their lives. They never forget that early sense of wonder, of excitement, of possibilities, of natural belief in themselves that they can make things happen. No matter how many times they run into obstacles, no matter how many times they stumble and fall, they assume it's temporary and that eventually they WILL find a way to their goal. They pick themselves up and try again.

If you can catch the positive, uplifting sense of that can-do spirit, I promise that you can succeed in business, arts, government, science, sports, or anything else you may attempt. Successful people know, or eventually learn, that the biggest reward in life is not arriving at your final destination, but learning to take joy in the never-ending journey. As psychotherapist Sheldon Kopp put it, "There is beginning, but there is also persevering–that is, beginning again and again and again."

Of all the resources that can make you a Maverick Millionaire, this brand of optimism, perseverance, and joy in learning are the some of the greatest assets you can have.

Chapter 9:

Good Mentors are Invaluable

One of the greatest adventure stories of all time features two characters that I relate to very personally. The tale opens with a young man who never knew his father (a fact which has certain echoes in my own life). In this case, the father went off to war and was never heard from again. Twenty years pass, and nobody knows if the father is alive or dead.

Meanwhile, the young man grows up and comes of age in a single-parent household. He's very unhappy with his mother, who is spending all her time with unsuitable boyfriends and letting the place go to rack and ruin.

In steps an older, wiser man with some sage advice.

"Listen to me, young fellow," says the older man. "Instead of moping around here with these no-account lowlifes, why not go in search of your father and try to find out what happened to him? If you find your father, you can bring him home. If you don't find him–or if, God forbid, you discover that he's dead–at least you'll have made a name for yourself as a responsible young person. When you return home, you'll be in a better position to take charge of things around here, and to help your mother straighten out this mess."

The wise counselor tells the younger man how to plan his trip…who to take along on the journey…and where to begin the search. He also provides some all-important encouragement. "I know you can do it, young man! You have the right stuff to succeed in this mission!"

So begins one of the immortal quests of world literature: Homer's *Odyssey*. The young man's name was Telemachus. His father's name, of course, was Odysseus (also known as Ulysses). And who was the wise old counselor, the fellow who took Telemachus under his wing?

> He was the original Mentor.
> That was his actual name, Mentor.

For the last 2,800 years, experienced people who coach younger people have been called "mentors," after Homer's great character. In *The Odyssey,* Mentor is actually Athena, the goddess of wisdom, in disguise. This plot twist is entirely appropriate, because if you find a good mentor in your own life, it's a gift from the gods…a gift of priceless wisdom, experience, and guidance. And, just as the original mentor was both male and female, both old and young, mentors in your life can be of any demographic.

I relate to this story in a very personal way because mentors have been such a huge part of my own life and of my success. I have been fortunate to have many mentors. Policemen and businessmen. Pilots and pastors. Young and old. Men and women.

Simply stated, mentors are **invaluable**–priceless beyond compare–because they can share the benefit of their experience. Mentors have already been through several courses in The School of Hard Knocks, and have learned many important lessons. A good mentor can offer guidance, advice, wisdom, encouragement, and even a bit of motivation. A great mentor can totally transform your life.

Anti-Mentors

To fully appreciate the power and value of a mentor, it's a good idea to consider the influence and impact that your friends and associates have on your life generally. It's hard to overstate the influence of those around you. In school, you may have hung around the smart brainy kids who got good grades. If so, you probably got good grades, too. Or, you could have hung around the pot-smoking crowd. If so, you probably smoked pot, as well.

If a mentor is someone who gives you wisdom and encouragement, then the opposite of a mentor is what I call a "crab in a barrel." Have you ever seen what happens when several live crabs are placed in a barrel or bucket? Each crab tries to escape by climbing up the side of the barrel. But as one crab moves up, the other crabs will latch onto it and drag it back down as they try to climb out themselves. The process becomes an endless, self-defeating cycle of pulling each other down, again and again. In the process, they prevent a single crab from escaping.

Sad to say, nearly identical behavior can be seen among human beings in many pockets of society.

On the surface, the siren song of the Crab People can sound deceptively tame: "Don't spend another night working. Relax, you deserve some downtime…and don't forget your old friends." Such talk may sound friendly or innocent at first, but it doesn't require much effort to see what often lies beneath the surface: negativity, fear, jealousy, and resentment. To some extent, such emotions are simply part of human nature.

- Negative thinkers will predict that your quest for success is doomed.
- Fearful people will tell you that by tempting fate, you'll only make things worse.
- Jealous people will feel that they deserve what you have (even if you worked for it and they didn't).
- Resentful people will be angry that you started from the same place they did, but achieved more desirable results–because they will take your success to be an implicit criticism of them.

When you hang around with these Crab People, you strongly increase your chances of failure. If you do fail, and especially if you give up after one or two failures, the Crab People will secretly be happy about it. Your experience will confirm to them that they were right not to make any effort, and they were right not to break out of their old routines in the first place. Misery, as they say, loves company.

If you want to enjoy success in life, you must give this factor very careful consideration. From the earliest moments of your quest for success, unless you are surrounded by unusually mature people who will not resent your achievements, you may find that you face a painful choice: to part company with negative influences or to give up your dreams.

After you begin to succeed, you will face another equally important choice. You will have to decide whether you are willing to work with unethical people who run roughshod over others to get ahead, or whether you prefer to go the extra mile, to achieve your success with integrity. This applies to your friends, your business colleagues, and yes, even to your mentors. Not all mentors teach the straight path! If a mentor invites you to go down a crooked road, you have to decide whether the lessons you might learn, would be worth the costs you will inevitably pay.

I have faced all of these choices from very early in my life, and I continue to face them every day. I chose to deliberately separate myself from bad influences during my school years. Later, as I learned the ropes of the real estate business, there were several occasions (and there continue to be fresh occasions today) when I parted company with cheats and liars who invited me to cheat and lie along with them.

I know that the decisions I made about who I chose to associate with had a direct, cause-and-effect impact on my success. These decisions continue to have a direct impact on the quality of my life today.

How to Find a Great Mentor: First, Make a Good Friend

How do you find a good mentor? You may not be able to get an appointment to see Bill Gates. Unfortunately, you cannot just walk up to a multimillionaire and say: "Hello, Mr. Millionaire, you are my new mentor. Please teach me what you know." But chances are excellent that you can find a way to spend quality time with somebody who can teach you how to catapult yourself (eventually) into Bill Gates' circle!

By the same token, a multimillionaire cannot walk up to any person on the street and say, "Hi, I'm Joe Millionaire. I want to teach you how to become wealthy." It doesn't work that way. Most people resent advice, no matter how good, unless they asked for it first.

In my experience, most mentor relationships begin as friendships. More than 10 mentors have impacted my life for the better. All of them become my mentors through friendship. I did not suck up to anyone, and I did not pester anyone to teach me all that they knew. I simply expressed a sincere interest in what they had to say, and before I knew it, friendships blossomed—often unintentionally.

Probably the single most important mentor in my life is Bill, a policeman I met at age 14 when I was reporting a property dispute. This big-hearted man took a liking to me and took me under his wing. He taught me the values of positive thinking and self-respect. He also taught me the power of boiling situations down to their simplest elements, and the technique of tackling big challenges one small step at a time. All of these things are invaluable tools that continue to provide the foundation of my life today.

Another crucial mentor for me was a real estate professional I'll call George. I met this eccentric genius through my aviation sales website. George paid for some of my early flying lessons, introduced me to aerobatics, and later he suggested that I move to Las Vegas and enter his profession. When I arrived, he taught me the ins and outs of the private money lending business, partly from a love of sharing what he knew, and partly, I believe, from the desire to have a worshipful young admirer.

Unfortunately, George entered on a problematic and painful time in his life. He began treating clients in an unethical manner, even though he always justified his behavior by claiming the client had done him wrong first. I asked George a very direct question: "What happened to the man who taught me never to cheat or shortchange a customer?" He didn't like hearing this. Eventually, I decided that our mentor-student relationship had to end. It was painful because our friendship ended, too. I'll always be grateful for what George taught me, but I have never questioned my decision.

A third great mentor was and is Tom, my first boss in the mortgage lending field. Tom taught me the basics of the business and the rudiments of effective self-marketing. Tom is also the man who challenged me to start my own company on the night of my 21st birthday. Today, Tom and I remain good friends and we continue to provide each other with brutally honest–but constructive and supportive–feedback. Tom also continues to give me advice and encouragement when I ask for it (and sometimes when I don't).

All of these wonderful folks became friends at first, and then later became mentors, because I chose to spend time with people I wanted to emulate. I felt I was becoming a better person by being around them. So, finding a mentor is a matter of approaching someone whom you genuinely admire, and treating them with an attitude of respect.

Friendships, as we all know, are not engineered. They develop naturally based on seeming coincidence and personal chemistry. That's why you will probably not be looking for a mentor when you find one. Setting out on a Sunday afternoon to find a mentor is not a realistic mission any more than setting out to find a friend at a specific time and place is a realistic mission. If you are aware of your surroundings, and if you place yourself in situations where opportunities may present themselves, then you are on the right track to finding both friends and potential mentors. (And when you meet them, it won't really be a coincidence, even thought it may appear to be.)

You may be wondering: why do successful people act as mentors to others? What does the guru gain from this relationship? Simply put, the mentor gains satisfaction from teaching what he knows. This, happily for all of us, is also a universal part of human nature. At our best, each of us has a need and desire to share what we love with other people.

If a successful person sees that you have a true desire to learn, most will take pleasure in sharing what they know, as long as they have a well-mannered and down-to-earth listener. It is almost like asking a pilot about flying. Once you ask a question and they are convinced that you're really interested, it is difficult to get him or her to shut up for hours afterwards. Pilots have such an intense love for what they do that they could talk for hours!

A Good Mentor is a Coach, Not a Pack Mule

Not all who ask for guidance are good students. Some of them want the mentor not only to point the way to success, but also to do the work for them and to hand them the results on a silver platter. This is not the role of a true mentor!

A good mentor is a coach: he offers success strategies, and gives encouragement. Both contributions are vital. The essence of a mentor relationship is about benefiting from another person's experience, but that benefit is not solely intellectual–how to do something with the best odds of success. It is also emotional. The mentor says: I have been there, I know what I'm talking about, and I say you can do it! The student reasons: "If my mentor says it, it must be true"…and he gains the confidence to try.

Mentors are people you can go to with your failures. You can say: "This is what I did, I thought I did everything right, and this is what came out of it…and I'm so disappointed I could cry." A good mentor looks at you and says: "Well, Jordan, let me tell you what you did wrong and how to fix it." They can point out what they would have done differently.

Sometimes, you can't see the forest for the trees. Sometimes you are so close to your own life, or your own career, that you look at an effort that didn't work and have no clue why it failed. You say: I can't see anything I would have done differently. In this situation, a wise mentor might say: "Yes, I tried that once too and had the same result. Let me tell you how I overcame it; this is what I would have done differently." Suddenly you move to a totally different perspective. You have new information and renewed confidence.

Many people assume the mentor relationship is strictly for young people or beginners, but I believe "mentorship" can and should continue always. I certainly hope so, because I am determined to continue learning all through my life, and I am committed to continual growth. There will always be people who know more than I do about each new field I try. And, just as I offer my own knowledge to those who sincerely ask for it, I am delighted to know that my future mentors will carry on this wonderful tradition.

Thousands of years ago, the original Mentor not only encouraged young Telemachus to go in search of his father; he also helped Odysseus win the battle to reclaim his rightful throne and restore peace to the kingdom.

Truly, a great mentor is heaven-sent!

Chapter 10:

Study Millionaires, Then Do What They Do

I have studied successful people my entire life. And when I say "studied," I mean I really put them under a magnifying glass. Whenever possible, I peered deeply into their lives and acted exactly as a nosey in-law would–asking questions, probing for details.

Behind the façade of apparent success, I often discovered people who made large salaries but spent it all on fancy cars, big homes, designer clothes, lavish vacations, and other things that they wanted but didn't need, or things they felt gave them status. These people often tended to be driven, insecure, and worried. (With all that debt that wasn't producing revenues, who wouldn't be worried?)

Next, I found another group of apparently "successful" people. Certain individuals have become multimillionaires because of their extraordinary business savvy, but they don't do business in an ethical manner. An aura of deceit and destruction hovers over their personal lives and their professional lives alike. To me, these people don't seem very happy, and I wouldn't call them truly successful.

Finally, I found people whose success was the real deal. These people worked hard and worked smart. They excelled at business and investing, or simply at life. They were honorable, ethical, and honest with themselves and with others. And, I found them in all walks of life. For some, success meant making a million dollars. For others, it meant creating a loving home and family. For still others, it meant flying the most demanding aerobatic routines in the world's most high-performance aircraft.

These are the people who I have found to be the healthiest and happiest–and isn't health and happiness the true definition of success? All of them were content with what they had, yet all were striving to make things better, too.

In this book, I primarily concentrate on monetary success, but it is entirely possible, even probable, that my focus of success will change as I grow older. But since my own success so far has been most notable in business, and since most of you are probably interested in financial success as well, most of the examples I give will be from that field. However, I hope you realize that the same lessons apply equally well to other areas of life!

It should not come as a revolutionary idea to say that if you want to be successful in a certain field, study those who are already successful in it–and then, do what they do! If you want to become a millionaire, study millionaires and emulate millionaires.

On the other hand, what may be surprising is just how far you should go with this emulation technique. It's not enough to emulate your role models in broad, general terms or to follow their example in the form of abstractions such as attitudes and ideas. If you really want to succeed, you should find a good role model and then follow him or her down to the tiniest details of dress, communication styles, where and how you live, and many other factors.

In any "role" that I play in life, whether in business, or social activities involving business, I adjust myself to each person or situation that I encounter. The best business people in the world are "chameleons." By definition, a chameleon is a lizard that can change its color to match the orientation of its surroundings, staying completely camouflaged in any situation. In business, you need to change yourself to your surroundings.

We all do this subconsciously already. For example, in a fine restaurant's dining room you probably act a bit differently than you would when sitting at your own dinner table at home. You adapt to your surroundings. Personally, I have to deal with clients of all ages. From 18 year olds to 85 year olds, I have to adapt my personality to fit each situation in order to convey a positive image.

The skills of a chameleon are something that you must begin to master early on in your quest for success. This is not to be interpreted as "change yourself and put on acts to please certain people," but it is to be taken that you must show different parts of your personality and use your talents to adapt yourself to the circumstances that you will encounter. Simply learn when and where to use your various personality characteristics.

A word of caution: what I do NOT want you to think is that you should become whoever or whatever you feel would serve the situation best. Selling yourself out and becoming someone you are not will never serve the greater good. In the process of emulating successful people, you must never sacrifice your values or your personal identity. Choose someone to emulate whom you admire and feel comfortable with. Someone whose values are in harmony with your own. That way, your emulation remains consistent with your core identity, and you preserve your most valuable resource of all: your inner integrity. Be who you are, and you will shine. Be someone you are not, and you will barely glow.

But once you find that right role model, get in gear with an aggressive program to follow their example in deeds as well as words and attitudes. That's right–we're back to ACTION again. Only this time, we are prescribing a highly specific set of actions that apply no matter what type of success you seek.

To Be Successful, First Look the Part

Do you believe that the way you dress can positively or negatively affect your success? Most highly successful people will answer that question with a stern "absolutely!" When you walk the street, do you judge the wealth and success of others around you by what they wear, how they dress, or even what kind of car they drive? As shallow as it may sound, most people do. Subconsciously, people relate how you present and take care of yourself with your ability to perform any given specific task. It may not be fair; it may not be right; it may not be accurate. But it's the way the world works.

We're always being told, "Don't judge a book by its cover." However, booksellers admit that that is exactly what the vast majority of buyers do. It is a well known fact in the publishing industry that a book or magazine with an attractive blonde on the cover (especially if she's portrayed against a red background) will sell far more copies than a book or magazine with identical content but, say, a house or landscape–or even a cute brunette–on the cover.

Why? Because people put great emphasis on appearances. Our culture promotes a double-minded attitude toward judging others by these relatively superficial standards. So, at the same time that we're told not to judge a book by its cover, we are also told "What you see is what you get." Under the circumstances, it's best to err on the side of caution in the matter of your appearance. Study those who are in the position you would like to be in, and then go and do likewise.

Two dramatically different examples from the entertainment industry prove this point. One is the well-known tale of how young Steven Spielberg infiltrated Universal Studios back in the late 1960s. He took the usual tourist's tour of the back lot–but instead of gaping at movie sets and TV production crews, he took careful note of the executives–how they dressed, what kind of haircuts they had, what sort of briefcases they carried. Then he came back the next day looking just like that, and claimed he had just been hired.

Spielberg looked "right," so the guards at the main gate let him in. He found an unused office, got into the circular list for company memos, and got a friend who worked for Universal to obtain an official gate pass for him. By the time management realized that upstart kid Steven Spielberg wasn't an actual company employee, he had wormed his way into the corporate culture. The rest is history!

A very different example of the impact of image on career success is a fellow we'll call "Alan." He is a very successful executive in the video game industry.

Alan is a wiz at crafting deals that involve new advanced technologies and applications. He has worked for some of the biggest corporations in the world. Alan likes his job, but he claims that what he really wants to do is *design* video games.

Unfortunately, despite Alan's superb track record, few of his fellow executives take his expressed wishes seriously. Perhaps the reason for this should be obvious. Video game designers tend to wear jeans, tee shirts, and sneakers. (They might even have pizza stains on those tee shirts.) Video game designers often have long hair, too, or at least shaggy hair. But Alan, who comes from a very proper British background, wouldn't be caught dead looking like that. He favors dark, pinstriped suits...handsome silk ties...white or pastel dress shirts...and gleaming black shoes. Alan's short, businessman's haircut is always tidy and his face is always well barbered.

No wonder this buttoned-down fellow has a tough time getting anyone to see him as a video game designer. Alan just doesn't look the part!

I have personally experienced "image discrimination" countless times, and often still do. In my case, it's also a form of age discrimination. As a particularly young businessman, I often faced negative scrutiny from older peers and potential clients because of my age and youthful appearance. To make matters worse, I have always looked even younger than my real age. It's bad enough to be 19 or 20, but it's even worse if (like me) you physically looked like a 14-year-old at that age!

Early in my career, I actually made this problem worse for myself because I "dressed like a kid." My credibility was diminished for this reason, even though my capabilities far exceeded those of many older competitors. Through the coaching of my mentor "George," I came to realize that the way people dress really does matter. When I started following his advice and wearing dark suits, white dress shirts, silk ties, and shiny leather shoes, it made an immediate difference in how people treated me. Today I usually dress like a 50-year-old CEO, but I still get comments on how young I look. However, the clothes clearly help take the negative edge off my youth.

Since image–and specifically clothing and haircut–plays such a big part in how people perceive your trustworthiness and competence, why not turn the fact to your advantage?

Dressing for success is simple and does not require hundreds of dollars in clothing and/or make-up. Instead, it requires thought and creativeness in making yourself look professional, no matter what your occupation, position, or ambitions. Early in my career, I shopped at discount stores and found off-the-rack slacks, shirts, and $10 silk ties. I often patronized a store called Ross' Dress For Less where I acquired good (expensive-looking) clothes at a fraction of the prices that are charged for virtually identical items in retail designer stores. You will discover that spending a little money on clothing and appearance can take you a long way in terms of credibility and salability of yourself.

Always overdress for the occasion. It is better to show up looking better and more formal than necessary, than to show up underdressed and feeling awkward. Contrary wise, it is never acceptable to under dress for an occasion. If this sounds like overdoing it, remember it is much easier for you to take off your tie than it is to go home and change into something more appropriate for a business or social event.

Does Sheepskin Equal Greenbacks? Not Necessarily.

If you're going to emulate millionaires, I think it's worthwhile to find out their views on education and follow that guidance, too. For much of the 20th century, a college education was looked upon as the necessary ticket to success in America. Parents constantly told children that a college degree was absolutely mandatory for success in life. Even today, our government still spends millions of dollars each year promoting the message that young people should "stay in school." These campaigns always point to reams of statistics that show people with a high school diploma earn much more over the course of a lifetime than people without one. Other statistics prove that people with a college degree earn still more.

I don't doubt those statistics for a second. The value of higher education is provable in dollars and cents. At the same time, it's vital to realize that this education must be supplemented by what you learn outside of school. You want to achieve a level of success that is outside the ordinary...and for that, you need to learn important lessons in the School of Hard Knocks.

This great truth was the theme of one of my favorite books on success.

Rich Dad, Poor Dad: What the Rich Teach Their Kids About Money—That the Poor and Middle Class Do Not! was written by Robert T. Kiyosaki and Sharon L. Lechter. Kiyosaki's father had an advanced degree but found it tough to make ends meet. Meanwhile, his best friend's father was eighth-grade dropout...and a multimillionaire. Kiyosaki paid close attention to his "poor dad's" lessons and was able to retire a very wealthy man at age 47.

My own experience has a certain parallel to this. Most of the people I know who make $200,000 per year and up do not have college educations. But they do have a permanent seat reserved in that famous classroom: the "School." Let me quickly acknowledge that an academic degree can be very helpful in some ways. Indeed, certain professions absolutely demand a diploma in that field. If such is your desire in life, more power to you.

If your desire is to become independently wealthy, the fastest route is probably self-employment. For that, no degree is ordinarily needed. Regrettably, some people (like Kiyosaki's biological father) spend lots of time and money to earn a degree, and some are taught theories that they have to "unlearn" later in order to succeed in the business world.

For myself, I just haven't had time yet to attend college. My mentor "George" advised me to get my degree later in life, more for fun and cultural enhancement than as part of my career education. And I may just do that!

The Basic Tool for Becoming Wealthy

Emulating millionaires also means following their approach to the all-important subject of *money*. It takes money to make money. But if you don't have money to start with, where do you get it?

Most people who become fabulously wealthy, do it with "OPM"–Other People's Money. In fact, this principle is the beating heart of capitalism: leveraging your assets, using whatever you have–cash or property–to borrow more money that you can invest and make more money on. And when I say "invest," I don't mean playing the stock market. I mean putting resources into a business venture that you control, grow, and profit from.

Using OPM is the indispensable catalyst to becoming huge from a company standpoint. You must have capital, and the chances are you are not going to have it on your own, so you must use OPM. Part of the basic premise of the success of Microsoft, Oracle and other high-tech companies is building on investment capital, often raised through a public stock offering.

Yet, thanks in part to all the publicity about high-profile IPOs (initial public offerings), combined with basic economic illiteracy on the part of so much of the public, there are many, many misconceptions floating around out there about start-up capital.

The first misconception is that you need a huge pile of money to start a company. Second, if you can't get this bankroll from a bank, you should try a venture capital firm. Third, and completely in contradiction to the first two, is the notion that using OPM is somehow morally wrong, or that being in debt is necessarily an evil.

Wrong, wrong, and wrong again!

Let's tackle the last myth first. Using OPM is far from immoral; it is *extremely moral.* Borrowing capital is one of the most moral things on earth! A good deal brings profit to both parties, and it also creates benefits for the society at large.

However, there is a big difference between good debt and bad debt. Good debt is money invested in a project that has a reasonable chance of returning a profit. Bad debt is money squandered on lifestyle. In other words, good debt is active or productive, while bad debt is passive or consumptive.

As for myth number two, we've heard a lot in recent years about venture capital firms. The concept of a finance company that will put big resources behind an unproven but promising idea is certainly appealing. However, venture capital is not the best place for most startups to raise funds. To start with, most VC firms want to buy a controlling interest in any company they invest in. That reduces the company founder to the status of an employee who can be undermined, overruled, or even fired.

Finally, it may take money to make money...but it doesn't take a fortune to make a fortune. Believe it or not, the great majority of emerging businesses in the U.S. are "bootstrap" firms that begin with under $1,000 in capital. Their real assets are not cash, but a great idea and the businessperson's own smarts and hard work. Eventually, if they need major infusions of capital, these companies get it from private investors or banks. Or, if they're in a hurry or have some other special requirement, they may seek an alternative type of financing. But they generally don't get their funds from VCs.

Examples of companies that began with less than $1,000 in capital are easy to find in virtually every industry. I'll avoid the obvious dot-com Internet examples and cite some more-traditional types of companies.

¢ Jose Serrato began his Dallas contracting company by scraping together $400, which he used to buy a broken-down old wall sprayer. Within five years, Serrato Drywall was generating annual revenues of more than $1.5 million.

¢ John Ford launched BarCharts Inc., a publisher of quick reference charts, in Boca Raton, Florida with exactly $1,000. A decade later the company's projected annual revenues were $10 million.

¢ Lori Bonn Gallagher also started her jewelry retail business with $1,000. At first she found exotic pieces from Paris to Moscow and sold them to retail outlets, eventually becoming a supplier to Nordstrom's. Today, Lori Bonn Design Inc. creates its own unique jewelry from its swanky digs in Beverly Hills, California.

¢ Greg Boyer began his Hawaiian landscape design company with exactly three physical assets: a pick, a rake, and a shovel. He had zero clients. Today he is the "landscape artist to the stars." His company works *for* the biggest names in the entertainment industry, and works *with* Hawaii's hottest architects and developers. Boyer himself lives at a Hawaiian dream estate, including a fantasy garden that he designed himself.

¢ John Schnatter cooked up Papa John's International out of the back of his father's Kentucky tavern with a start-up cost of just $1,600. (Okay, so it's not a grand or less, but it's close.) In 2005, annual revenues for this popular pizza restaurant chain were right around a tasty $1 billion.

Most Millionaires Invest in Real Estate

In an earlier chapter, I stated that this book won't be about real estate, and it isn't. But while we're on the subject of emulating millionaires, let me briefly point out that most millionaires eventually get involved in real estate as a way to protect their wealth. This is true even if they generated their wealth from entirely different markets, and it's true even if their careers remain focused on entirely different industries.

According to some estimates, the wisest and wealthiest investors use real estate as the anchor of their portfolios, carrying as much as 80% of their assets in real estate or business. The rest is distributed among stocks, bonds, mutual funds, and CDs. In addition, the better hedge funds frequently tout the fact they invest a substantial portion of their assets in real estate as the most stable part of their portfolio.

Why do sophisticated business people consider real estate so valuable and attractive? Because experience shows real estate is the best long-term investment available. There is absolutely no other long-term investment commodity that you can reliably buy for a relatively low cost, then resell in 10 or 20 years and retire on the profits. Yet we see average people doing exactly that with real estate today, all around the country...and it's been that way for 150 years.

"Long term" is the key concept here. When you find a place that you think is an opportunity, that value can go up tenfold over time–or more than tenfold. We've recently seen properties here in Las Vegas appreciate 100% in a single year. Real estate also offers considerable tax advantages under current federal and state laws. For all these reasons, I think real estate is absolutely better than stocks or CDs as a place for wealthy people to park their money.

These facts are a major part of the reason that I decided to make my own career in real estate. Again, I studied what millionaires do, and then I went and did likewise. If they invested 80% of their assets (cash) in real estate, I thought it would made sense to invest 80% of my own assets–time and effort–into the same market. So far, the track record of my company has not proved this strategy wrong!

Millionaire Outside, Millionaire Inside

Obviously, this chapter is an explanation of what millionaires do and how you can benefit from following their example. But in a sense, this entire book also fits that description–since the author is a multimillionaire himself. But in these few pages, I simply wanted to stress that it's not only strategy and tactics that you should take from millionaires. If you want to become one of them, the fastest way to get there is to think like them, act like them, dress like them, and live like them.

As the old saying has it, the clothes make the man (or woman). I think that's true, and it's also true of thoughts, habits, and every other detail of career approach and personal lifestyle.

When you've got a template that works, use it!

Phase 2:

EVALUATE Your Maverick Business Plan

In ground school, I was not a whiz kid. To tell the truth, I hated the book-work and the rote memory of airspace rules and mathematical formulas. I liked understanding aerodynamics–but beyond that, I just wanted to escape from the dusty classroom and go fly.

Once I climbed into the cockpit with an instructor, taking actual flight lessons, I began to learn viscerally what ground school teaches intellectually: what it feels like to experience lift and gravity…takeoffs and landings… turning and banking…stalls and recoveries.

I loved it. I discovered that flying came naturally to me. For example, when it came to landings, once I got the basic technique down, I would get in a groove and just squeak those tires right on the tarmac and roll them precisely down the stripe in the center of the landing strip.

Experienced pilots talk about the need for constant, relentless vigilance in the air. You have watch dozens of things at the same time – the wind, the weather, the engine, your altitude and attitude, the compass, other airplanes, and many others. You must constantly guard against anything that might go wrong…and there are a million things that can go wrong, any of which can be fatal.

It is a tremendous amount of work.

Yet learning this is a matter of making them part of you, part of your body, part of your mind, part of your instincts. Once you have learned the basics, you can go out and conquer the air…and have a hell of a good time doing it.

The Power and the Glory

And now let's talk about "the art of the deal." If you think about it, we all make deals, and we make them throughout our lives. If you're a star athlete signing a contract, you are making a deal. If you're Mr. Average Joe, whenever you buy a new car or negotiate the terms of a new job, you are making a deal. When you say, "Honey, will you marry me?" you are pitching a deal!

Actually, those are just a few of the larger deals we might make in our lives. The fact is, we all make dozens of smaller deals, too, on a nonstop basis.

For example, when you and a colleague agree on how to divide up the responsibilities in a joint project, you're making a deal. When you and your spouse agree to visit one set of in-laws for Thanksgiving and the other set of in-laws at Christmas, that's a deal, too. (And a great bonus clause would be: "Then for Easter vacation, let's get away to Hawaii just by ourselves.")

So no matter what decisions you make, deal-making is a fundamental tool for success in life. This chapter won't give you the nuts and bolts of how to negotiate or brainstorm a good deal (that comes later; see Chapters 24 and 25). But this chapter will teach you how to lay a solid foundation for any agreement you make in your life.

A solid *ethical* foundation, that is.

You must go forward with every deal you seek, confident that you are in the right. Every single deal should be built upon a sound basis that will last. That's how you nourish a healthy, positive relationship between you and the other party.

The way to attain that confidence and to create that sound basis is through ethics.

I define ethics as doing something that helps you AND that helps everybody else around you. This runs contrary to the belief that many businesspeople have, that a good deal means taking the other person (or the other company) for all you can get. But I believe that is a shortsighted and ultimately *self*-destructive approach.

To see why this is true, look how this one-sided bargaining works in the context of, let's say, a personal relationship. If you do something with your spouse that is good only for you, is that a wise thing to do? Absolutely not, because only one person is benefiting. It is a completely selfish, very short-term, ignorant approach. In the long run, it's not good for the relationship.

On the other hand, if a particular deal helps the person across the negotiating table, but it doesn't help you–and if it also doesn't help your team, your suppliers, your colleagues, and everybody else around you–is that a positive thing to do? No, and for the same reason as doing something that's only good for you: it can't last.

Giving away the store may make some people feel virtuous, and it's quite true that ethics and morality are often presented in terms of self-sacrifice and altruism (caring only about the other person, nothing about yourself). I strongly disagree with this philosophy and in fact to me, such a program is extremely UN-ethical. As I see it, if you're constantly depleting your reserves of time, energy, or capital, eventually you will have nothing left to give. Then somebody else will have to take care of YOU. Where's the virtue in that?

The rule of thumb in business is that a good deal is one where everybody wins. That's true, but there's more to it. I say that when both sides win, it's not just a matter of profitability and mutual advantage; it's a matter of honor and of ultimate morality, too. The win-win scenario is moral because it serves the greater good. When two people (or two companies) make a truly good deal, it's not just good for them–it's good for everybody who works for them. It's good for everybody they work with. Eventually, as these positive benefits ripple out into wider circles, it's good for society at large.

In business and in life, I look for a win-win scenario in every deal that I do.

Putting My Client's Money Where My Mouth Is

Not long ago, an 80-year-old lady came into my office to apply for a loan. She said: "I'm in foreclosure and I need help. In three weeks if I don't make my mortgage payment, I will lose my home and all the equity in my house. I need you to give me a loan, secured with my home as collateral."

After getting the details, I said: "Lady, you don't want to borrow money from my company. Why, it would cost you a ridiculous amount of money to go through me to get a loan. After all, your payment to me at a 12% interest rate would be three times your current payment. You are paying $600 a month and you can't make the payment now. If I make you this loan, how on earth will you make a payment to me of $1,800 a month?"

She simply repeated her problem. "I'm going to lose my house," she said. "If you just give me the loan, I can pay it," she promised. She was desperate and only thinking of solving her short-term (three-week) problem. She was not thinking realistically about her long-term problem.

I considered my options. On the one hand, if I made the type of deal that this poor woman believed she wanted...and if by some miracle she managed to make her payments to me...I had an opportunity to make $5,000 cleanly and legitimately.

Realistically, however, I had a chance to make a lot more. It didn't take a crystal ball to foresee that she would soon fail to make her payments, and then I could foreclose on this poor woman's property. Her house had much more value as collateral than I would be lending her. So, I could make the deal, take her house, and sell it for a very nice profit.

I took a step back and said to myself: if I lend to this lady on the terms she suggests, I am a predator. I'm no better than a loan shark or anyone else who takes advantage of others.

In this situation, some people would make the loan and justify it by saying, "If she's stupid enough to take this deal, it's her own fault." Perhaps so, but that is not my mindset. If we did it her way, I was going to win significantly, but she was not going to win at all. So I told her the truth.

I said, "Look, ma'am, if I give you this money, you'll lose your house to me. That hurts you, obviously. To be honest, I could not foreclose on an 80-year-old woman, so if I write this loan and you don't pay me back, then I've only hurt myself. This whole situation does not make sense."

She said no bank would give her a loan! I said you're absolutely right. She asked what she could do. I suggested that she sell her home. She said, "But it's a one-story home. I can't live in apartments–they all have stairs."

The woman was right about one thing: she was in real trouble. She needed help and I wanted to give it to her. I went into deal-making mode...which, remember, to me means going in search of the win-win scenario.

I said, "Okay, ma'am, here's the deal. We both have needs to be met here. I need to make a little bit of money out of this. You need to do something with your house in the next 20 days or you'll lose it. So here's what I'm going to do. You will sell me your house at a 15 to 20% discount. By paying off your existing mortgage and buying the house from you, in return I'll put $50,000 into your pocket. You can use that money to get another place to live, someplace that you can really afford."

She repeated that she didn't want to sell, but again admitted that without help she couldn't possibly make her mortgage payments.

So I showed her how much I would make under the terms of the deal that I proposed. After buying and reselling her home, I would gain a 10 to

15% margin after my other costs. To make it easier, I said I would find her a ground-floor apartment with affordable payments and easy physical access, in a decent part of town. With her profits from the sale of her home, she would be able to pay many months of rent...a bit more than her expected actuarial lifespan required, in fact. However, I realized this scenario still represented a risk down the road: if she lived into her 90s, she would again be out of money and facing homelessness.

I presented the woman with a second option that I felt could eliminate that risk, too. I explained that what I do is invest money in real estate trust deeds. "Instead of banking that $50,000 from the sale of your home," I suggested, "invest the money with me. I promise that if we get into a position where it's a bad investment and you need to get out, I'll buy you out of it–but that will never happen." I pointed out that by investing her $50,000 in a way that generated 12% annual interest for her, she would receive $500 a month...income that would cover her monthly apartment rent in perpetuity.

She agreed to this deal. To me, it was a great deal because we both won. I won because I made $50,000 or $60,000 out of the agreement. She won, because she is still an investor with my company who gets her check every single month, without fail. I found her that nice ground-floor apartment, and she never has to worry about her living situation again. It is a total win-win situation. She's happy and so am I.

The Most Moral Thing Is Also the Most Practical Thing

In one sense, this story represents a special case, because I was able to provide life-changing help for a vulnerable senior citizen. But in another sense, this story is not unusual at all. I approach every single business deal in the same spirit: how can we both win? How can I do good for my client and for myself? This approach makes both of us stronger. It brings me a short-term profit...builds a long-term relationship with a repeat customer...generates positive word of mouth ...resulting in referrals that turn into more clients and more deals...and, no small matter, it also makes me feel great.

In recent years, American citizens have seen many examples of bad faith, greed, and lawbreaking in the highest financial circles. The Corporate Hall of Shame has had to build a new wing for companies like Enron, Worldcom, Global Crossing, Adelphi, and many others. The leaders of these companies believed they could lie, cheat, and steal their way to success.

In the short term, perhaps a few pirates at the top can enjoy champagne and swimming pools this way. In the long term, this unethical and illegal business philosophy not only preys on the lives of employees and business allies alike…it also represents a one-way ticket to "Club Fed" (federal prison) for many CEOs. That is exactly where they belong. Greed is not only socially destructive, ultimately it is self-destructive.

Corporate raiders and rip-off artists have lost sight of what the art of the deal is all about. Misguided altruists, who sacrifice their own interests in the belief that it's somehow good for society, have also missed the point. A deal is an opportunity to create a *mutually* profitable, *mutually* nourishing, *mutually* sustaining, long-term relationship.

The most moral thing you can do, turns out to be the most practical thing you can do, too. Begin your journey on the road to success with this lesson firmly in mind, and you will go far!

Chapter 12:

Not All Markets Are Created Equal

Before you launch any new venture–in business or in life–one of the most important lessons is to learn that not all markets are created equal. A success strategy that works wonderfully well in Market A, may just be "so-so" in Market B only 10 miles away. And it could be a total flop in Market C in another state or region. Also, a success strategy that works in one year or decade, might not succeed in the same geographic location during a different era or decade. Conditions change. Customer bases grow or shrink. New products and services pop up to replace old ones. New competition arrives, turning once-promising, wide-open markets into unattractive, over-served markets.

All this adds up to one thing: in the words of the old song from Broadway's *The Music Man*, "You gotta know the territory!" There is no such thing as a foolproof, universal, one-size-fits-all plan for surefire success in business or in life. Each venture must be carefully customized for its time and place. Therefore, one of the "commandments" in business is, know your market...preferably *before* you invest all your capital and years of your life trying to make a certain enterprise work in a particular industry.

This is a good place to give another one of those all-important "what not to do" warnings. Many people have a tendency to identify markets that aren't really there. For the sake of turning a profit, or for the sake of doing something they think they will love, they try to make a market appear out of nowhere. Ninety-nine times out of 100, it doesn't happen. Even the one time it does happen, the odds are 99% that it won't work very well.

Enthusiasm Is No Substitute for a Solid, Well-Researched Market

A man called me recently and said: I have this great idea for an invention. It's going to be huge. You can get in on the ground level; I just need $100,000 to get started. I politely said thanks for the opportunity, but that's not what I do. However, this would-be inventor insisted on giving me a demonstration. He was so persistent that I finally agreed to give him a few minutes of my time.

He came to my office, I signed a Non-Disclosure Agreement, and he revealed his great new product. Obviously, having signed the NDA, I can't say what it was. But let's just say it was the equivalent of a water filter tester...and it was a heavy, awkward contraption that you wear on your back. The inventor envisioned this as a commercial product that would be used in several different markets. "Look, the tester can go from sink to sink and check the quality of the water, on the spot!"

What he left out of the equation was, do these commercial sectors really want this product or service? Would they really buy such a peripheral item? Would they pay a high price for such a machine that provides marginal service? Couldn't the same goal be accomplished better, more cheaply, and more easily by tackling the situation another way? Would the prospective clients even have a budget for it? If they did have a budget, what method were they using to address the issue now? Why did they end up going with that method? If this idea was so great, why was nobody else doing it?

Inventors tend to answer that last question with, "Because I am a genius and nobody thought of my idea before." Sometimes that's true. But most of the time, the fact is their invention is a terrible idea. I don't mean to pour cold water on all creativity and inventiveness; far from it. But five minutes or five months of market research can save five years of headaches, heartaches, and failure.

MAVERICK MOTIVATOR:

Create your own opportunities! The Bureau of Labor Statistics projects the self-employed category will grow 5% from 2004 to 2014, compared with 2% growth for the decade that began in 1994.

When choosing your market, don't make the error of turning a hobby into a business. Aspiring artists probably should not run an art supplies store; aspiring musicians probably should not run a musical instrument store; and prize-winning gardeners probably should not run a nursery or a garden supply store. This is especially true if the prospective entrepreneurs believe their love of the hobby will translate into an equal love of running a business that focuses on that activity.

Yes, it's an excellent idea to go into a field that you're passionate about.

But anyone who thinks a hobby-centered business will be as much fun as pursuing the hobby itself, has a painful lesson or two coming. The truth is, running the business is an entirely different discipline than pursuing the hobby. It won't feel like painting or music or gardening, it will still feel like business: finding products, seeking customers, making sales, handling accounts receivable, and all the rest.

Even if you find a profitable market niche for your hobby-based business, the sheer act of putting the business aspects first will probably come to interfere with your love for the hobby. After spending all day selling art supplies to artists, talking to artist customers about their art (not yours), and so on, when you finally have a bit of free time (which most start-up business owners don't have anyway), the last thing you'll want to spend those precious moments on is thinking about the same subject to which you've just devoted an 80-hour workweek!

I learned this from my first successful business, an online aviation parts brokerage. It made decent money, and it taught me some vital business lessons. But after a while, I realized it was starting to take the fun out of the whole world of aviation for me. It was turning a pleasure into a chore. Flying as a commercial pilot turned out to be just another variation on that same theme.

As Mark Twain once explained (in the famous story of Tom Sawyer and the whitewashed fence), "Work consists of what a body is obliged to do. Play consists of whatever a body is not obliged to do." Don't ruin your hobby by turning it into a chore.

Choosing a Market With Proven Potential

Market research before launching a company requires not just learning your customer demographics, but also learning the usefulness, the need and demand, that your intended market area or population will have for your specific product or service. How do you acquire this information? Begin with a simple survey of businesses in your trade area that are similar to the one you're thinking of starting. Start with the phone book! Or start with the Internet. Read. Make phone calls. Talk to people who are already involved in the industry.

Ask these questions:

Are there any businesses around already that resemble the one I'm considering? Why or why not? If such businesses do exist, have they been established for a long time? Are they successful and well-respected in the community? Again, why or why not? Does there appear to be room for one more business of this type in the market? Does the planned market area have a growing population or some other factor that spells growing demand that could support a new venture? If it's already a well-served market, what about my business or service will be distinctive, unique, and put me into a strong competitive position?

Next, go to your local library or bookstore. Read everything you can about your proposed market and business. This won't make you an expert, and it won't provide all the answers for a sound business plan. However, it will knock off a bit of the ignorance that any greenhorn is naturally prone to.

Third, attend some seminars and conferences that focus on your proposed business. If your idea is truly a promising venture, there will probably be professional trade associations that cater to your industry. Find out what they are and attend their events. If you have to wait six months, fly across the country, pay for a hotel room, and pay $1,500 to get in the door, do it. Attend every seminar that seems relevant to your proposed business.

Just as important, network like crazy while you're at the conference. Introduce yourself to people who are already in the business and ask their advice. (Naturally, be polite and don't take up too much of their time.) You can learn priceless knowledge from your own on-the-spot "consultant" who will give you a seasoned, canny perspective like nothing else out there. You might even spark a mentor relationship that will provide invaluable guidance through the entire course of your business career.

When choosing a conference, make sure it's one aimed at professionals who are already in the business, or that it's taught by a strong team of professionals who have already established a top reputation in the business. Stay away from seminars taught by mid-level executives or nobodies, catering to a roomful of wannabe's. These are a waste of time and money.

Any investment that you make into quality seminars and conferences will be worth 10 times, 50 times, or 100 times in knowledge gained, compared to what it costs you in time and dollars. Remember, before you  launch a business is when time, money, and self-education are relatively cheap and have the most effectiveness. After you launch a business, it's 10 times harder, 10 times more expensive, and 10 times less effective to make fundamental changes.

Once word gets out that you are thinking of starting a business, you may receive solicitations from custom market research service firms. Once you actually launch your business, you'll be flooded with such offers. I get them all the time. The pitch always goes the same way: "We've been servicing your industry for many years and we know the territory. We can help you increase sales and target your marketing."

Everyone makes this claim. I've investigated these market research firms and I don't recommend them. Basically, they sell data–a very simplistic service that usually comes at a very high cost. To me it's not worth it if what you're getting is a high-priced, generic set of generalized statistics that pretends to be customized to your specific company or your specific market area.

However, in addition to seminars, industry conferences, and trade shows, there are two types of paid market research that can be very valuable. One is buying a pre-existing market study from a *reputable* firm. For example, Marketdata Enterprises Inc. is a publishing company that offers publicly available business analysis about various niche markets. Their comprehensive reports include estimates for national receipts by the industry over many years, typical start-up costs, operating expenses, ratios, emerging trends, franchising, challenges, competition, opportunities, and much more. Each study costs a few hundred dollars. But this type of product, from a reputable source, can provide invaluable business intelligence to help you decide whether you should enter a certain market, and if so, how.

The so-called "feasibility study" can be another good market research tool. This is especially valuable for retail firms, probably less so for services companies (although even there, it might help in some cases). If you're thinking of investing $1 million of your own money into a retail business in a certain city, it's a good idea to spend at least $50,000...a comparative pittance...on having a professional feasibility study performed. In fact, if you are contemplating such a large investment, you'd be crazy NOT to have such a study done. If you hope to get bank financing, any responsible lending institution will probably make it mandatory.

For your feasibility study, choose one of your industry's top experts, someone with a sterling reputation, to perform the study for you. Ideally this will be a person who not only does feasibility studies all the time for high-profile clients, but also a person who is active in this business himself–and who lives or dies by the accuracy of his research. Ask for a client list and letters of recommendation. Then give them your business plan and let them do their magic.

In a few weeks, you should receive a goldmine of data: what is your realistic geographic market area; who is your competition; what specific types of products and services will be successful (and which ones won't); what is your customer demographic; how should your business be slanted to appeal to that demographic. In a retail store environment, for example, the best experts can even tell you, to the penny, how much money per square foot each department of the store will generate in a particular market. They can provide truly expert recommendations for which niches to target and which to avoid.

How to Really Clean Up in Your Chosen Market

Let's say you were considering entering the commercial carpet and floor cleaning business, for example. You have heard that it's a low-tech, recession-resistant industry with a low entry cost and over 500,000 small, mom & pop companies. This industry also includes billion-dollar corporations that specialize in managing large buildings, but at the local level these are unlikely ever to replace most of the mom & pops for various reasons. You've also heard that this industry has enjoyed double-digit growth for years at a time.

From reading a good market survey, you would learn that all of these promising descriptions are true. You would also discover that finding and keeping employees who are legally in the country is a huge headache. You would learn that employee turnover is higher than 200% each year...not a good sign. You'd learn that the industry offers no upward mobility. And you'd get an early warning about campaigns to unionize janitors working for contractors in certain cities or regions, but not others.

Then, if you attended the annual conference for the home and commercial cleaning industry, you might learn that what was once a low-key, backwater business has recently attracted lots of MBAs and PhDs who are tired of endless layoffs and have decided to start their own businesses. You would learn that in some local markets, the phone book has gone from five pages of cleaning businesses to 20 or 30 pages in the last five years. You would discover that cutthroat competition is eliminating all but the largest and most aggressive, or the smallest low-ball, bottom-price outfits.

Now, should you enter this business? As with so much else in life, the answer is "It depends." Perhaps your city hasn't been flooded with competition yet. Maybe you have a chance to buy an established firm with a solid reputation and a steady client list. Perhaps you don't care about upward mobility, because you are content to run a small yet steady business. Or maybe you plan to create your own "upward mobility"–growing your empire through expanding to other cities and buying other cleaning firms. Maybe the labor situation in your region is unusually good for some reason.

If all of these factors were true, entering the cleaning business might be an excellent move.

Different Is Good! When to Ignore the Experts

Just because I recommend doing extensive market research, please don't think I'm saying you should let "experts" decide your destiny for you.

Above all, please don't think I'm saying that you should stick with formulaic, cookie-cutter business concepts. Far from it!

If I had followed that cautious path, I never would have opened my own company. In Las Vegas, private money lending firms were few and far between when I started my company. Another negative factor was that the private money lending industry had a spotty reputation in Las Vegas, thanks to some inept local "practitioners" of a bygone era.

However, I knew the local real estate market cold from my prior years as a mortgage lending officer and as a real estate investor myself. Thanks to my online aviation parts business, I understood the concept and technique of being a broker–how to bring together buyers and sellers. Some potential private lending clients knew me and wanted my services. The risk factor was low, because start-up costs were minimal and if things didn't work out, I could always get another mortgage lending job. Finally, one more crucial factor argued for entering this not-so-obvious market: my mentors unanimously agreed that I should go for it.

Some of the craziest and most offbeat business ideas you've ever heard of have proved to be wildly successful. Some were carefully researched, but I have to admit many were happy accidents. How about gourmet treats for pets? Or what about specialty food items for pets with allergies? Both concepts have become huge winners for various entrepreneurs.

But while the specific niche may have been unproven, the overall market is a winner. Americans spend $30 billion per year on pet food. Providing something unique or slightly different *within the larger context of a solidly established, already-proven market* can sometimes be a great strategy, even if some well-meaning experts try to talk you out of it.

Newlyweds Jennifer Melton and Brennan Johnson launched the Cloud Star Corporation in San Luis Obispo, California when they were both in their 20s. She was a structural engineer; he was the marketing director for a clothing company...and their dog Samantha was a picky eater with a delicate stomach. They launched the company on a shoestring, but word of mouth led to an explosion of company demand. Four years after the company began, it was turning over more than $6 million in annual sales.

Did this couple listen to the nay-sayers? Absolutely not. "People thought we were crazy," Jennifer laughs. But they started with a very low initial investment, so their risk was minimized. And although they didn't know much about their market at first, they researched it quickly–and in depth–before putting any real money into the company. As Brennan explained to *Entrepreneur* magazine, they created databases of health-food stores, gift stores and pet supply stores nationwide. Quarterly mailings were sent to those potential customers.

What made the difference between success and failure in this case? As one nay-sayer asked Jennifer, "Everybody claims to have the best dog bone; what makes yours so special?" The difference was a unique yet appealing product that didn't exist on the market before Cloud Star offered it to the pet lovers of America. But again, the U.S. pet food industry grosses tens of billions of dollars, each and every year! Jennifer and Brennan were entering a market with proven profit potential. They simply carved out a niche and provided what that niche needed. Also, with such a low initial investment, this couple had the freedom to be flexible and to revamp their business according to what they learned. So, they grew based on success.

Like pet food, sunglasses are another surprisingly huge market in this country. Ken Wilson launched Gatorz LLC with an investment of just $75 and one catchy claim to fame: he made his stylish eyewear from strong yet lightweight aircraft aluminum. "We [try] to come out with something that no one else has," Wilson explains. Thanks to a powerful yet unusual product (and some savvy marketing that began with the motocross and hip biker crowd), Ken racked up more than $15 million in sales in just a few years.

Identifying what you can do that's different...how you can do it better than anybody else...and what differentiates you from the other guy...is crucial to the success of any business in a competitive market. It's called a "unique selling proposition," or USP, and most successful individuals and businesses have one.

Success in business, then, is a matter of understanding your market and *also* understanding your own strengths and how YOU can fit into that market.

Chapter 13:

The Art of Talking

"Salesman" is often perceived as a dirty word in the English language, as in "used car salesman." "Saleswoman" and "salesperson" aren't much better. We all know the stereotype. From the customer's viewpoint, a salesperson is a flashy, fast-talking sharpie who will say anything, promise the moon, and sell his or her grandmother to make a buck.

Surprisingly, from a business viewpoint the salesperson's reputation is often not much better. Because the sales function is so vital to the lifeblood of most organizations, the sales team frequently includes the highest-paid members of the staff. Yet, salespeople are often perceived (sometimes justly and sometimes not) as doing the least work of anyone in the organization. The combination of high pay and (allegedly) low effort helps explain why salespeople are frequently among the *most resented* members of the organization, as well.

No wonder the mere mention of a salesperson puts most people on the defensive!

Unfortunately, as in so many professions–from politicians to (lately) priests–a handful of bad apples seem to define the image for the entire group. Of course, good salespeople never push customers in an unwanted direction. True sales professionals don't waste your time (or their own) convincing you that you need something that you actually don't have any use for. A great salesperson shudders at the very thought of badgering a prospect until he finally buys.

I often hear people say, "I wouldn't be good at selling. I'm not a good salesperson." They are absolutely right, of course. This statement is a self-fulfilling prophecy of the worst order. Anyone who would say such a thing is, by definition, a TERRIBLE salesperson. (Or, in a few rare cases at the other extreme, a person who says this could be a very slick article who is poormouthing himself, in order to disarm a prospect.) Myself, I wouldn't hire anyone who called himself a terrible salesman. I have neither the time nor the inclination to attempt to motivate someone who says, "I can't," regardless of whether the subject at hand is sales or anything else.

So here is our next maverick lesson. You are already a salesperson, whether you like the idea or not! But here's the great part: if you truly understand what being a salesperson means, you'll soon come to love it.

Let's begin by clearing up the misconception that we have any options in this matter. In business and in life, we all play the part of a salesperson at one time or another. In fact, the more ambitious and successful we are, the more of a sales function we assume. We sell our goods and services to our clients, of course, but that's just scratching the surface. Look a little deeper and you'll quickly realize we also sell our ideas to our colleagues, our partners, and our employees. And, as noted, we sell ourselves to–well, just about everybody we come in contact with. Our bosses, potential bosses, colleagues, clients, potential clients, vendors, spouses, friends, you name it.

When a cop stops you for speeding and you turn on your most charming smile and give out a cheerful "Good afternoon, officer! I know I was going a bit over the limit, but I have this really urgent doctor's appointment"...you had better believe that you are pitching a sale!

The most important sale you will ever make is the sale of yourself. In my experience, the most successful sales effort begins with integrity–meaning, YOUR integrity. If a good deal is a win-win scenario, then a good sales pitch is your offer and intent to provide genuine service to the client.

If it doesn't help the customer to buy it, then believe me, you don't want to sell it. We constantly meet potential investors who explore what we have to offer right up to the moment when it's time to commit, but they say, "You know what? This doesn't sound like my type of deal." My response is: "You may want something more aggressive, or more conservative. That's totally okay. If you ever want to diversify, please give me a call first." And we leave it at that.

When YOU'RE Talking, you're selling.
When THEY'RE Talking, they're buying.

The above words are an old saying in the sales game. I learned the truth of this old saying almost by accident, long before I ever heard the saying itself. Back in the days when I sold airplanes for a living, I once found myself representing a seaplane. At the time, I was desperate for a commission. So as soon as I got a live customer in my grasp, I began hyping the aircraft for all I was worth:

"This is such a cool airplane!" I gushed. "Seaplanes are so great! It's awesome to own a seaplane, because you can fly out to these beautiful, remote spots in the middle of nowhere, put down on a lake and go fishing and camping! Now let me tell you about all the features of this plane–"

The more I talked, the less the prospect wanted to listen. He was agitated and aggravated. Everything about him said loud and clear that he didn't want to be sold. I couldn't understand why I was having such a hard time. Finally I got tired of beating my head against a wall and, by dumb luck, I did the smartest thing possible: I gave up.

That's right. I gave up. I stopped "selling" the plane and let the conversation go a different way. I shut my mouth and let the customer talk about whatever he wanted to talk about.

Of all things, the guy started talking about...seaplanes. He was eager to demonstrate that he didn't require lectures from anyone, much less a teenaged kid like me. "Oh, I know all about seaplanes," he said. "I've got 5,000 hours in seaplanes. Hell, I used to take trips up into Alaska in a seaplane. Let me tell you about it..."

Then I did the next smartest thing: I continued to shut up. He continued to talk. You can guess how this conversation turned out. In the course of recounting all the fun he'd had fishing on Alaskan lakes with a seaplane he'd once owned, the man worked himself up to a fever pitch of enthusiasm. He finally wound up by saying: "You know, this really might be a fun airplane for me to have. It's more than I wanted to spend...But, you know, sometimes you just have to splurge. That was a helluva lot of fun back then. Let me talk it over with my wife and I'll call you back."

The next day, to my utter shock, he called me back and said he was sending me a deposit. Had I sold this man a seaplane? No, he *sold himself a seaplane!* All I did was present the opportunity and (eventually) get out of his way. I had been trying to sell him so hard, that I really didn't care what he wanted or needed. But the minute I shut up and let him talk about what he wanted and needed, he decided this seaplane was EXACTLY what he wanted and needed.

I learned a tremendous lesson from this experience. After I entered the real estate business, my mentors reinforced the lesson by elevating it to the level of principle. *The best sales technique is actually a process of letting people convince themselves.* If you have to "sell" somebody on something, it's probably not the best thing for them. The product or service should sell itself. And if your product doesn't fit that person, you move on. The world is full of good prospects. If one doesn't buy, the next one will–or the one after that.

That means (as discussed in the previous chapter), half the battle is finding a good market, a great product or service, and finding the right customer demographic. Then you bring prospect A into contact with product B...step back...and let the magic happen.

How to Handle the "Tough" Prospect: DON'T!

A "tough prospect" is somebody who is not ready to buy, or who has numerous objections. How do I handle them? I don't. When someone is dead set against something, by "handling" them, you'll turn them off. The harder you work to convince them, the more they'll scramble to find additional objections, more justifications not to buy.

In this situation, the most effective move you can make is to practice a sort of psychological *jujitsu*: stop talking. Just become a listener, a conversationalist, or even agree with their objections. The moment you do this, the entire dynamic of the conversation suddenly changes in your favor. In the Bible it says: "Agree with thy adversary quickly." I have found this is brilliant sales strategy, because it totally surprises and disarms the prospect. Let me give you an example from a typical conversation in my own business life.

Prospect: Hey, your company is new. I don't know if I want to invest with you, because you might close up shop one day–and then I've lost my money!

Jordan: I have to be honest with you, you're totally right. You're thinking the right way: how to protect your investment. And you're also right about the fact that we're a new company.

(And then…I stop talking. I leave it at that. The customer expects me to make an argument. I politely decline to oblige. After a moment, the customer blinks in surprise and says:)

Prospect: Don't you have anything to say about it?

Jordan: Not really. We're a new company. You said it yourself.

(And then, I shut up again. I smile pleasantly. I wait. The ball is in his court. I have all the time in the world. I let the prospect decide if–and when, and how–to make the next move. Surprisingly often, at this point he lobs a soft serve.)

Prospect: Well, I guess each deal stands on its own. What do you have to offer?

(I answer that question briefly, and before you know it the prospect starts to overcome his own objections.)

This is how to make a sale: you're honest, you're forthright, and you're not trying to sell them anything. You're just presenting an opportunity and they're free to take it or leave it.

Above all, you're not trying to prove the prospect wrong. If someone has an objection–and the "tough prospect" is belligerent about his reasons why he doesn't want to do business with you–then if you try to turn it around, you are proving them wrong. If by some miracle you "succeed" in proving them wrong, he'll only get angry and walk away. Some success! *"A man convinced against his will, is of the same opinion still."* You may have won the battle, but you have lost the war.

(So, when clients give you objections–especially objections that may have a grain of truth in them–instead of arguing, agree with them! Align yourself with them. Put yourself on *their* side. In fact, eliminate the whole notion of "sides" from the conversation. This immediately throws the prospect way off balance. Why? Because by instantly agreeing with your "adversary," you take an objection that they think is an insurmountable barrier to doing business, and you defuse it. By acknowledging it without giving up and walking away, you have non-verbally communicated the message: "Maybe we can still do business.")

This leads us to the art of listening.

The World's Most Under-Used Skill! (Why Real Listening Is NOT the Same Thing as Just Waiting to Speak)

Listening is the most under-utilized skill in the world. Often it seems that everybody has something to say about virtually every subject under the sun, whether they really know a darned thing about that particular subject or not. But how many people are eager to listen?

When we hear an opinion that we disagree with, most of us are overwhelmingly tempted to blurt out our own views. We want to say: "I strongly disagree with that and here's why." However, giving in to that impulse is egotism and immaturity in action. It blocks your chance of creating a bond with the other person...which means, the relationship never gets a chance to take hold.

(When I praise the art of listening, I don't mean passively sitting and impatiently waiting for your turn to talk. That's not listening; it's merely conforming to the polite rules of social interaction.

No, what I am advocating here is a very active, intently focused form of listening. Lower your barriers. Let go of your judgmentalism. If the other person voices opinions that you don't agree with, allow those opinions to simply wash over you and flow past you. Don't react to them. In fact, don't even focus on the opinion as such. Instead, focus on *the person who is speaking.* Focus on the person *behind* the opinion.)

The true art of listening is to be willing to get yourself in a space where you are relating to another person, above and beyond your ordinary typical self or your ego. It means moving into a "zone" of commonality. True listening creates a mysterious and powerful dynamic because apparently, on the surface, you are not "doing" anything. But in that seeming passivity, you are actually doing a great deal.

If you learn to practice this type of receptive, non-judgmental listening, you will be offering the other party a powerful form of validation of their personhood.

Please understand this: in active listening, you are NOT validating their OPINIONS...you are validating THEM. There is a world of difference. Even if you disagree with someone, by listening to them and not passing judgment on their views (or at least, by not expressing judgment), you have validated them. You are silently saying: you are worthy of respect. You are worthy of a full, fair, sympathetic hearing. You are worthy, period.

This type of validation doesn't cost you anything. On the contrary, when you give somebody that silent message of validation and respect, it is incredibly empowering. It empowers YOU, precisely because it empowers the other person!

Giving both silent and spoken validation means that from the very first moment of your interaction with the other party, you have put the relationship on the basis of "I am going to serve you." This is true whether the other party realizes it or not. Therefore, from the very first moment of active listening, *you have taken control* of the relationship.

If you understand the true power of this dynamic, then you realize there is an ethic of service in just listening to someone who needs or wants to talk. You are actively doing something for that person. Again, since service is what your entire sales relationship will eventually be based on anyway, by offering this form of validation, you are making that relationship shift into operation on this "service basis" instantly–from the first moments of your interaction.

When you finally do take the lead in the conversation, you have already given yourself great credibility, because you have already defined the relationship. You have defined it as one of service–almost before you even opened your mouth.

When It Really Is Your Turn to Talk...

Naturally, you can't have a conversation where the other person does 100% of the talking. Although you should put the emphasis on listening, that doesn't mean you should be silent as the Sphinx. Sooner or later, you have to say something. The question is, what should you say?

While I'm listening, I am also thinking: is this person voicing a need that I can help to meet? Are they identifying a problem that I can help to solve? If so, when it's appropriate for me to take the conversational lead, I will point out that perhaps I can help meet that need or solve that problem.

But even this is done in a dialog-oriented format that honors the principle, "When you're talking, you're selling...When they're talking, they're buying." In other words, when it's really and truly time for you to do some of the talking, don't treat it like an opportunity to hog the floor and make a longwinded speech. Your turn to lead the conversation is not the time for monolog; it's your time to co-create a productive, carefully directed *dialog*.

You can accomplish this by offering some innocuous questions that gently prompt the other party to do some more talking. Only this time, they're talking on your agenda...and you're subtly guiding them to a certain conclusion. Your agenda is getting them to state a need, and the conclusion that you're driving toward is for them to recognize and acknowledge, in a non-resisting way, that you as a salesperson have a product or service that can meet that need.

Simple as this sounds, it is the difference between "making a sales pitch" versus "having a real conversation." You can put thoughts into people's minds in a way that makes them feel they thought of it, rather than feeling that you forced a particular conclusion down their throat. In fact, you can evoke certain thoughts to put the ideas or issues that you want to bring up, into their heads. Then...by golly...they will bring it up for you. I have spent quite a lot of time trying to perfect ways to do that. This approach takes longer than simply blurting out your points. No doubt about it, this is NOT the most direct method of communication. But for that very reason, it is by far the most effective method in a one-on-one situation.

Let's examine a concrete example of how this might work. Suppose I'm a new car salesman and you have just walked into my showroom. After a casual welcome, the first thing I do is–back off and give you space. Meanwhile, I also let you know that I'm available if you need or want to talk to me. In other words, I immediately put YOU in charge of the tempo of the relationship, if there is going to be one.

Here's how the conversation might go:

Jordan: Hi, welcome to Jordan Motors. How are you doing today?
You: Fine. I'm just here to look around a little bit.
Jordan: Okay, great. Feel free to roam all over the showroom. My

name is Jordan; I'll be over there if you have any questions.

(I'm polite, professional, non-invasive. I have put you at your ease.)

You: Thanks.

(Now I walk away and leave you to look at the cars and the stickers. You can see me in the distance, but I don't watch you and I don't "hover" in any sense. Inevitably, you have some questions. You call for me or otherwise get my attention.)

You: Hey, Jordan, can you...?

(I walk over.)

Jordan: Sure, what questions can I answer for you?

You: You know I really like this car; can I take it for a test drive?

(I still don't assume you want to buy the car. I don't start telling you it's perfect for you or why it's such a bargain. Instead, I respond to your agenda...and then I shut up.)

Jordan: Absolutely, let me go grab the keys. And by the way, your name is...?

You: Sam Jones.

Jordan: I'll be right back with those keys, Sam.

(When you came back from your test drive, I avoid the typical manipulative sales ploys. I don't ask: How did you like it? Isn't this a great car? Can't you just see yourself in this baby? I also **don't** *say: Man, this car suits you to a "T"! In addition, I don't wear out your first name by calling you "Sam" every two seconds. Instead, if you have specific questions, I answer them. The car comes in these colors; it has these options; etc....Finally, if you indicate continued interest, I begin to ask some gently leading questions–with the emphasis on "gently.")*

Jordan: So what do you do, Sam?

You: Well, I'm in information technology. Sales and marketing.

Jordan: Uh-huh. What kind of car do people need in your line of work?

(Notice, I didn't even say "what kind of car do YOU need." I keep the discussion in the realm of theoretical, impersonal information, not in the realm of "qualifying a prospect.")

You: Well, I have to make a good impression on the clients, so I need an upscale, professional-looking vehicle.

Jordan: I hear you. Kind of like "dress for success"...only in this case, it's "You are what you drive," huh?

(In this case, all I did was validate your statement by feeding it back to you in a slightly different form. Psychologists call this non-directive interviewing.)

You: You got that right. A lot of guys in my company own this model and they really like it.

(Bingo. You, the prospect, have just pitched me a huge softball. But I don't try to knock it out of the park! I don't say, "Yes, everybody loves this vehicle because blah, blah, blah." Instead, I remain in a service mode. I keep asking low-key questions.)

Jordan: Really? That's interesting. What do they like about it?

(You, as the prospect, now go on to do my job for me. You list all the features and benefits that the other guys in your office are always bragging about–the great gas mileage; agile cornering and maneuverability; whatever. I'm nodding, silently validating what you say. Meanwhile, you're selling yourself this car.)

Jordan: Yeah, we hear that from quite a few of our customers. *(Once again, I'm validating your points.)* So what do you think?

(This is a very open-ended question. It could mean ANYTHING from "Do you agree with your colleagues about the excellent features of this car?" to "So, are you really in the market for a new car?" to "So, do you think you might want to drive this one home?" to "How about those Dodgers?" Again, I am leaving YOU in charge of the tempo of the relationship.)

You: I may be interested. I'd like to talk a little about price and terms...

Jordan: Sure, we can do that. Would you care to step into my office?

(And so we're off and running...)

Notice that the most important things in this conversation were never explicitly stated. As the automotive salesman, I never said out loud: "Hey, do you want to buy this car?" You as the automotive shopper/customer never said, "I want to buy this car."

Notice also that YOU, the prospect, verbally established the basic benchmarks of the conversation. I created a vacuum with my softball questions, and you moved into that vacuum with your answers. Specifically, when you replied to my prompt about your needs by saying, "I need a professional-looking car," we identified the basic nature of your need.

In answering that question as you did, you further acknowledged that "what you need" is "what I have to sell." I asked the question about your needs, knowing that you were going to say, in effect: "I need a car pretty much like this one." My implicit reply is: you just said you needed a car like this one? Funny thing is, I've got a car like this one to sell you. In fact, I can sell you this one right here!

During the entire course of this exchange, I have made you feel totally comfortable because I never put any pressure on you. I did not try to close you. I did not even try to pre-close you!

Instead, I just stayed in that relationship and attitude of giving service. If you wanted to make a statement I listened, and invited you to elaborate, if you felt like it. I didn't push my points; if anything, I pulled your thoughts and concerns out of you.

Likewise, although I took control of the relationship by defining it as one of service, I never took command of the *conversational agenda*. Instead, together we created a zone of freedom and genuine interchange–and it was that natural, unforced dynamic between us that invited you to keep moving toward me.

For all these reasons, it was easy and comfortable for you to be there in the showroom. And, as our dialog evolved organically at a pace that you were comfortable with, it became easy for you to gradually move toward making the eventual decision to buy.

At its heart, great salesmanship is service, and service is power. The ability to sell yourself, your company, and your product or service–without being blatant about it–is one of the most difficult lessons to learn. It cannot be faked. The spirit of service is genuine, or it's nothing.

This lesson is not just for career sales professionals. It applies to every walk of life and every person who needs to create a positive impression, communicate with other people, forge a bond, or persuade anyone of anything whatsoever. But the basic principles are the same in any situation you may face. Once you learn this lesson, it can help you go places you've never dreamed of.

Chapter 14:

Build Long-Term Relationships

Peter Drucker, the great management guru of the 20th century, often said, "The purpose of a business is to create new customers." That is a startling insight for many people who believe the purpose of a business is to make a profit, create a product, offer a service, or generate sales. But Drucker's definition includes all of those functions between the lines, while putting the emphasis where it truly belongs: on the relationship between a business and its customers.

If your products and services aren't the right ones, and if they are not supported by the correct sales effort, then customer relationships suffer and eventually, your company dies. So while sales are vitally important to your company, they are not your ultimate objective. Your ultimate objective is to create and sustain positive, successful relationships with customers–then sales will happen naturally as a byproduct.

In the previous chapter, we talked about defining the client relationship on the basis of service from its opening moments. This principle has a second part: if you believe in "service after the sale," you have waited too long to provide service–and you probably won't be making many sales.

Our earlier example of the conversation in the new car showroom (Chapter 13) demonstrated how it can work, when a single conversation is placed on a basis of service. Now let's see what it looks like when that same basis of service is extended to the *entire relationship* between you and your clients.

Every business relationship has its own rhythm and tempo. In part, this rhythm is determined by the type of service or product in question. For example, people don't do a lot of window-shopping and research before deciding to buy a McDonald's hamburger. But if you're selling anything less familiar (and anything more expensive) than a McDonald's hamburger, then you will probably find that your customers move through a series of stages.

Typically, these stages include a get-acquainted phase, an informational or educational phase, and a closing attempt or decision to commit. During this series of events, there is a natural, unforced rhythm as a person moves from an acquaintance, to a prospect, to a client. Depending on the particular business and on the individual customer, these stages may be spread over a series of meetings that can last for a single day, a week, a month, a year, or even longer.

For the purposes of this chapter, let's assume that each of these three basic phases represents at least one meeting. That often happens to be the case in my business; in your industry the rhythm may be different. But the point is to recognize that each phase has a goal and agenda of its own.

The Get-Acquainted Meeting: Earning Provisional Trust

A get-acquainted meeting can happen through several avenues. It can come through advertising, from a networking session of some kind, from someone reading a newspaper or magazine story about you, or from someone coming across your website...anything that prompts the potential client to get in touch with you.

The best way for a get-acquainted meeting to happen is as the result of word of mouth: one of my existing clients refers me to a friend. I try to do as much business as I can from such referrals. To me it's the best way to do business, because the first client has already made a positive evaluation of you if they pass you on to a potential second client. The prospect then begins the get-acquainted meeting in a receptive frame of mind, prepared to have a positive impression of you.

A get-acquainted meeting can even happen in a chance encounter. It does not necessarily have to occur in the office, a networking event, a marketing event, or within a business setting of any kind. It can happen anywhere. Suppose you strike up a conversation with a stranger at Starbucks. He looks like an investor, maybe he's reading the *Wall Street Journal,* and you start talking. That can be a get-acquainted meeting.

Actually, I prefer off-the-cuff conversations with people in a promising setting to just about any other context for a get-acquainted meeting. I prefer this because when these encounters happen spontaneously, there is absolutely no sense of expectation by either side. This lack of expectations, oddly enough, creates the perfect environment for the seed of a relationship to be planted–and possibly begin to grow.

The goal of a get-acquainted meeting is to establish rapport and thereby begin to create a foundation of trust. It doesn't have to be profound trust; after all, you're not asking the other person to put his or her children in your care. The goal is to earn provisional trust. You want to create the sense in the prospect's mind that you might be well worth talking to a second time, somewhere down the road.

You don't earn this provisional trust by showing up and saying, "Hi, my name's Jordan, I'm a multimillionaire, I own my own company." You do it by saying, "Hi, my name's Jordan, what do you do?" Dig into who they are and what they're all about.

After you demonstrate genuine interest in them, what their life is, if they are a genuine potential prospect, eventually they will turn it around 180 degrees and want to know more about you. When they ask about you, that gives you the opportunity to explain who you are and what you do in a tactful way: you are helpfully answering their questions, not pushing unwanted information at them.

The first rule of a get-acquainted meeting is, you don't close. Never try to close somebody at a get-acquainted meeting! Even if you have a product to sell them at that very moment, and even if you believe your product would be perfect for that prospective client, you don't offer it. You stay away from it.

The agenda for a get-acquainted meeting is just that: getting acquainted. You talk to them, you get to know them, they get to know you a little bit, and if it seems like the potential prospect might be interested, you end with: "You know what, I'll get back to you next week and we'll talk a little bit more." Otherwise you simply end with: "It was nice to meet you."

If you try to move beyond that, such as by suggesting: "Let's go to my office" or "Let's go to lunch," you are placing expectations on the slender reed of this budding relationship. Suggestions like these represent a half-close. Once you make such suggestions, you're no longer in a get-acquainted meeting; a new and more aggressive agenda has been introduced: "Let's see what we can do with each other."

I don't even like a half-close. If you so much as say, "I'll call you next week and we'll talk about what we do," that is a half-close. That is leading into, "I am going to try to sell you something." You don't want that, because at this point your prospect doesn't want that.

Whether it's "Nice to meet you" or "I'll get back to you," the correct ending sets up the second phase of your relationship: an informational briefing.

The Informational Briefing: Short and Sweet

An informational briefing is also NOT where the close takes place. But it is one of the best ways to get people *prepared* for you to attempt to close them. At the very least, it's a good excuse to call someone a second time.

When I have a client or prospect who is very important, or when one of my investment relations executives brings in a major investor for a get-acquainted meeting, we meet and talk, compare backgrounds, seek to generate some rapport, and find common ground. Then in a week or two, that common ground gives me a reason to call them with a piece of information (if something relevant turns up). However, that is the sole purpose of my follow-up call: to provide information.

As in: "Say, Lauren, you mentioned last week that you might be interested in an investment someday if a certain type of opportunity came up. Well, I just wanted to let you know that such and so has happened, and it occurred to me that this might be the type of thing you were talking about."

And then...you shut up. You let the other person ask their questions, if they have any. You provide the answers in a very brief, businesslike way. Again, you don't try to close. You don't impose any expectations on the meeting or the conversation. You're just there to help! Think of yourself as being in stand-by mode, like a fireman. If the bell rings, you'll spring into action. Otherwise, do nothing to frighten off the prospect.

By offering information in a non-pressuring way, you are building your credibility and you are building the relationship.

My company has an informational booklet, but I don't offer it or put it into the prospect's hands on my own initiative. They have to ask for it. On our website too, we have a choice of several ways that a prospect can initiate contact and select how we should follow up with them: e-mail me, call me, send me a package by mail.

If they ask us to send them the information package and we don't hear from them for several weeks, we call them and say: "Do you have any questions we can help with?" and "If you're ever interested in this type of investment, please keep us in mind." And that's it.

Again, let's compare this to what normally happens at this point in a new car showroom with the typical high-pressure salesperson. You ask for information, and the salesman starts pushing the product: "Wow, this is a beautiful car! You really need a car like this!"

In other words, you haven't been there five minutes, and you're already getting hustled. It is a completely unnatural action on the salesman's part, because there is no relationship between you. The stereotypical car salesman may try some obvious shtick to create ersatz rapport, but it doesn't work–because while he's asking about your kids, he's simultaneously writing down prices. That is not building a relationship; that is baloney. It is exercising phony sales skills.

The best way to close an informational meeting or conversation is to convey something like this: "Okay, I just wanted to let you know that such-and-such was out there. Call me if we can be of service, or if you have any more questions. Great talking to you...Bye."

The prospect hangs up thinking: "Gee, this guy was really helpful, and he didn't put any pressure on me to buy. I'll be very interested in his next phone call, too."

A Good Lead Is Self-Qualifying

The purpose of an informational meeting is for YOU to provide information to the PROSPECT. You don't ask *the prospect* to provide information to *you*. You don't want to qualify them for a sale at this point. You don't want to size them up, overtly or covertly. And make no mistake, people always know when they're being qualified–those prodding questions are an unmistakable signal! I certainly know when I'm being qualified. An investor comes to my office and says things like: "So you're a pretty young guy, ha ha ha...You do pretty well."

And I say: "Well, I do okay."

And you know they're waiting for you to say: "I'm 22 years old, or I'm 12 or I'm 98 years old," or whatever. When I don't say it, they hem and haw and finally come out with it: "Well, how old are you?"

This type of interrogation doesn't make me eager to build a relationship with someone. Whenever anyone tries to size me up in this condescending manner, I am completely turned off. I have people walk in my office all the time, look at me across the desk, and it's obvious what they're thinking: "Who are you to run this company? What exactly qualifies you more than others to handle my business?"

By the same token, if I ask a prospect a lot of probing questions about their finances, their history, their goals, their plans, and so on, it will be obvious that I am sizing them up, and they will be equally repelled.

Qualifying a lead happens all along during the course of a relationship. A good lead qualifies himself or herself. It happens in the get-acquainted phase; in the informational phase; and in the closing phase...but it is never an overt part of the conversation.

Instead, you qualify a lead by assessing the maturity and professionalism of their image and behavior. The key is–not making them feel like they're being set up to be sold.

Phase Three: The Non-Close Close

You have now gone through two full meetings (a get-acquainted meeting and an informational meeting) without attempting to sell anything. The reason for this reticence is quite simple: if you try to close someone right off the bat, or if you seem to have an agenda at any point, you lose face with that potential client. You communicate fear that they *won't* buy, and fear is always unattractive.

The best way to prevent people from thinking that you have an agenda, is not to have an agenda. You should go into the first, second, or third meeting, phone call, or contact, with the genuine position that you don't have an agenda and that you are not looking to close a sale. Timing of the close is therefore completely up to the prospect. In my business, you leave the close (if there's going to be one) to the third or even fourth, fifth, or sixth conversation.

At some point, probably in that third meeting (but often later), the time arrives for the sales pitch. I make it as little like a sales pitch as possible. If an investor says, "Okay, I've got a half-million dollars to work with," I wait for him to ask: "Do you have any deals available? How can I get involved?"

I reply: "Well, this paperwork needs to be filled out. This is the process we follow, this is how we do it."

Notice, in making this reply, I still didn't close! All I did was act as an administrator, an information provider. I answered the prospect's questions.

Any time that I have to "sell" something, in the sense of trying to persuade somebody of the product's or service's desirability, I'm very cautious. If any attempt at persuasion is necessary, it means you either (a) are not going into a win-win situation; or (b) you didn't set things up properly in the first place by creating a service relationship and providing desired information.

Thousands of years ago, the great Chinese general Sun Tzu wrote in *The Art of War* that the victory is won before the battle takes place. It is won in the minds of the victors. In a similar vein, the sale happens before the "close"–the battle is won before the combatants close ranks–the outcome is decided before the encounter.

If I do have to "sell" or persuade, I approach it from the point of view of the client's needs. I say: "Hey, Carl. You said you had some money to put into a project. I think I might have a deal that might fit what you're looking for–but I'll leave that up to you."

That's exactly how I do it. I quickly put the initiative back with them. That is a sales pitch, but it's one without expectations. Notice that there isn't even an implicit close. It's simply putting an opportunity out there; they can take it or not–and my world won't be rocked either way, because it's not a case of me having something that I "need" them to buy from me. It's me supplying something that they (might) need. This conveys confidence, and confidence is appealing.

In my business, particularly in the case of new clients, as many as one out of three has a "kick the tires" moment. They will say: well, I'd like to go look at the property that we would be lending on. I help them do this. I say: Hang on, here are the driving directions. They sit there thinking: "This guy really wants me to see this property. That must mean he's confident in it."

I don't accompany the prospect on the visit. What reason could I have, to be there to show them the property? They don't need me to point out the features. If the property doesn't stand on its own, the only reason I'd be there is to explain away some problem.

If I showed up, I'd be tempted to say: "Oh, I know the grass is a bit brown–but this property is really good, Carl!" It's a total sell job. I am not here to sell; I am here to let people buy. So, the fact that I am NOT standing by their side when they make the inspection is much easier for me, and it places less pressure on them.

A Good Prospect Sells Himself

Just as a good lead qualifies himself, a good prospect ultimately sells himself. And he does so at his own pace.

One year, my plane was at the Reno Air Races. One of the announcers noticed my company's name, spelled out in big letters on the wings of my airplane. He also noticed "12% Return" on the tail. This announcer came up to me after the show, pointed to my company name on the wings, and said: "Jordan, what is this all about?"

I said: "Ah, it's a real estate investment thing." And I left it at that.

He asked, "What kind of real estate investment thing?"

I explained: "We're a private money lender. We lend 50 to 60¢ on the dollar on properties, so we have very good equity position, and we're very easy on borrowers to qualify, so we charge a higher interest rate–which we pass on to our investors."

And I shut up.

He absorbs this and then he asks: "Well…how exactly does that work with borrowers and investors?" I explained a little bit further. He asked, "Can you send me some information?" I said sure.

When I got back to my office, I sent the package. Perhaps I should have called him a couple of weeks later to offer an informational briefing ("Did you get the information packet? Do you have any questions I can answer?"). But instead, I waited until we ran into each other six weeks later at another air show. I asked him if he had received the material. He replied: "Oh, yeah, I got it…I haven't had time to look at…I'll get to it."

I thought, okay, cool. I didn't hear back from him. At this point, again I probably should have called him for that informational briefing follow-up, but I didn't. I got busy and let it slide.

A year later, I got a phone call from this fellow. He says: "Jordan, how are you?"

I say: "Hey, long time, no hear. How are you?"

He says: "Yeah, listen–I read that book you sent me a couple of times; I've got some questions for you."

I say: "Okay, what are they?"

He asked some basic questions, which I answered–and then I left it alone. I didn't sell him, I didn't say: So, are you ready to invest now? I went into one of those artful silences that invite the other party to make the move.

He said, "Hmm. It sounds like this is kind of a neat thing. How do I get started?"

I said: "Well, you just fill out the paperwork and send in your money. We'll call you the next time an investment opportunity rolls around, tell you what it is, and see if you want to participate."

He said: "Hmm...That sounds good...Yeah, you know what, can I do that? Can I just go ahead and send in a check and you'll take care of it?"

Notice what has happened here. He's asking me to sell him a deal! He's asking to buy something. I didn't have to attempt a close. I say: "Oh, yeah, sure, no problem. Send in a check and we'll get the ball rolling."

A man, whom I had not heard from for a full year, sent me a check. Eventually he invested in a property and we began doing business together–but I didn't sell him the deal. He sold himself that deal. What I sold him was an understanding myself as a "service provider," not a "product pusher." Based on that understanding, he eventually asked me to provide the service that I provide.

Trust That the Timing Will Work In Your Favor

Do I care if a client's request for my services comes soon or late in the relationship? Not at all! It will happen at different speeds for different clients. Each client will choose the pace that's right for him or her. In the previous chapter, we talked about shifting the basis of a single conversation to one of service through validation. Now you have followed that same strategy through several meetings and shifted the entire relationship to one of service through information!

¢ We begin with the stance of: "I'm a service provider; not a product pusher."

- ¢ We created the self-qualifying lead by letting the prospect take the initiative.
- ¢ And we climaxed with the "non-close close," where ideally the prospect asks you to provide the service that you provide.

Now, that is a meeting rhythm that I can live with! I'm not interested in a short-term transaction; I am interested in a long-term relationship. That is where the best business comes from.

I actually didn't know I was going to solo that day. The afternoon began when my instructor, Mike, climbed into the cockpit with me as usual and had me take off as usual. We did some stalls, some steep turns, a couple of touch-and-goes. The next time I came in for a landing, Mike said: "Okay, let's make this one a full stop." I taxied in, and he said:" Just keep the engine running."

Huh?

Mike is unbuckling...He opens the door, climbs out of the plane, and stands on the tarmac. He looks in at me and says,"Okay! Go do three touch-and-goes and come back." Then he closes the door and walks away.

I knew it was coming, but it still felt like a shock. At this point, I am 16 years old, and I have barely a dozen hours' flying time under my belt. Am I really going to solo now? Okay! So I went down the runway...pulled back on the yoke...and I'm airborne.

I can remember lifting off the ground and looking over to the right seat, which is the co-pilot's seat–where the instructor sits. For the first time, it's empty. I remember thinking, Oh man! I'm up here on my own...nobody is here to help me if I get in trouble! I gotta get this thing back on the ground by myself! It was not a fearful moment, simply a defining moment of: Okay, this is all me. Sink or swim.

I flew a standard pattern around the airfield and brought the plane down, exactly as I'd done countless times before. Then I took off again and repeated the exercise two more times.

I loved every minute of it. Soloing felt beautifu–not only fun and freedom and exhilaration, but also a huge feeling of accomplishment.

I was up in an airplane, on my own! I was a pilot!

Chapter 15:

The Day I Become a CEO

After opening my company, we quickly zoomed from a brand new start-up to a highly profitable company with very strong revenues. I took our success for granted and began hiring staff I didn't need, spent unnecessary money, and failed to track where our revenues were coming from. I didn't have a clear picture of the "who-what-when-where-how" of our customer demographic or our sales. Instead, we were flying by the seat of our pants.

One day I woke up and said, "My company is hurting. We have not closed a single deal in 60 days. Our cash reserves have plummeted from six figures to zero. What's wrong here?"

I realized then, that my company didn't have any real structure. I hadn't taken the time to investigate *why* we had succeeded before. Where were our clients coming from? How could we encourage those clients to become steady, repeat customers? How do we replicate this process into a formal, company-wide system?

The day that I began asking those kinds of questions, was the day that I became a CEO. I even changed my title at that point from owner/president to chief executive officer of my company in order to remind myself that, as the head of my company, I had responsibilities that went far beyond merely processing the day-to-day, week-to-week, and month-to-month ebb and flow of business that came in (or didn't).

For one thing, I was responsible for the livelihoods and careers of all the people working for me. In addition, I was the only one within the organization who had both the responsibility and the authority to step back and look at the big picture…and I had better do it!

A Crisis That Comes in the Life of Every Company

The crisis that I have just described is a crisis of leadership. At one time or another, this crisis occurs in the life of almost every company. The problem is most obvious with start-ups, but it also strikes the largest, most successful companies in the world.

The basic diagnosis of the malady is that the company's top executive *continues to use the problem-solving tools and perspective that worked for him before he was put in charge of the entire organization.* He fails to shift his perspective–which means, he fails to promote himself to "commander in chief," with the job of setting the overall direction and deciding what systems, procedures, people, and sub-organizations will be put in place to ensure that the company moves in that direction and reaches its ultimate destination.

Let me give you two specific examples:

An award-winning chef opens his own restaurant. He spends 80% of his time supervising the chefs who now work for him, making sure the recipes are perfect and the food is top-notch. After all, it's important that every meal is excellent, right? But the restaurant owner–the CEO —doesn't pay enough attention to advertising and marketing, greeting the customers, making sure the dining room has an appealing atmosphere, making sure the bathrooms are clean, and establishing a financially sound food-buying process that allows the restaurant to offer quality meals at competitive prices. With this formula, the chef-CEO can offer the world's most delicious cuisine...and still go broke.

A brilliant engineer is promoted from vice-president of R&D to president of an established, 50-year old manufacturing company. However, she spends 50% of her time supervising the R&D department, almost as if she still had her old job. She never looks outside the company long enough to realize their competition is revolutionizing the industry–not with new technology, but with new customer service concepts and radical new forms of distribution.

Worse yet, this new CEO seemingly fails to notice or care that her department heads never really engage each other in genuine debate over this threat, or any other vital issue. Instead, the various departments continue running their own little "empires." Sure, they meet their budgets and produce their required individual results. But they never unite behind a well-considered plan of integrated action. Result: the company rolls out the best-engineered product of its history...and loses half its market share.

A Question of Focus: What is a CEO's real job?

This problem has been described as remaining an "operator" instead of becoming an executive *(The Effective Executive).* The problem has also been characterized as being promoted to the level of your incompetence

(The Peter Principle). Most recently, it has been conceptualized as remaining a technician instead of becoming a true entrepreneur *(The E-Myth)*.

Whatever you call it, the issue is focus: where does the CEO put his attention? The answer to that question depends, of course, on another question: how does the CEO define his or her job?

Simply put, the job of a CEO is to be the captain of the ship. This somewhat familiar analogy is actually quite precise, when you think about it.

¢ The captain/CEO sets the destination (goal) and charts the course (strategy) after consulting with his crew (department heads).

¢ He orders navigational course changes, tacking left and right if the ship runs into unexpected weather, unfavorable currents, or other conditions.

¢ He keeps an eye on the entire ship from stem to stern at all times, and continually orders repairs, upgrades, remodeling and even rebuilding when needed.

¢ He both motivates and disciplines the crew, but he doesn't do their jobs for them (unless it's an emergency).

¢ He makes small talk with the passengers (customers), but his purpose in doing so isn't trivial: he uses this input to get a fresh, outside perspective on how the voyage is going.

Lots of "operators," "incompetent Peters" and "technicians" sincerely believe that they are fulfilling all these functions, when in fact they are largely failing to do so. But the real test of whether a CEO is meeting these responsibilities isn't whether the boss "claims" he's doing his job. The real tests are whether the destination is wisely chosen; whether the vessel arrives there on time and shipshape; whether the crew is happy; and whether the passengers are seasick or refreshed at the end of the voyage.

(In other words, there are independent, objective measurements of the success of any CEO, beyond merely taking his or her word for it. The most important measures are revenues and long-term growth. If these tests are met, the customers are happy, the company makes a profit, the shareholders smile, the company becomes steadily stronger, and the CEO keeps his job. If these tests are not met, customers leave, profits plummet, shareholders revolt, the company becomes weak, and the CEO gets the boot.)

To put it another way, a good CEO is proactive, not reactive. It's his job to be satisfied with today's performance, if possible–but "dissatisfied on principle" with repeating that same performance (no matter how excellent) tomorrow, next quarter, or next year. That's because he knows that the market is constantly changing, and he knows that his company must continually change, too, in order to survive. Therefore, a good CEO is concerned with *creating* the future, not just *handling* present-day demands as they arise. Finally, a good CEO knows how to empower his team so that team members can give their best efforts and can realize maximum results, individually and collectively, from their performance.

> In short:
>
> An "operator," an "incompetent Peter," or a "technician" is focused on the *business* of the company. A CEO is focused on the *company*.

That is, an operator is almost entirely involved in processing mundane transactions. He is focused on making the products, providing the service, and selling the inventory.

A CEO pays attention to these matters, but from a certain distance–*and always within the relentless context of high-level strategy.* A CEO is focused on defining and refining the mission…creating and establishing the systems that will make it most likely for his team–not himself–to achieve that mission…and educating and encouraging the individual members of the team.

The remainder of this book will discuss many of these management components. Subsequent chapters will be devoted to company goal-setting and vision; team-building; leadership; meetings and internal company communication; setting and refining a strategy; making decisions; and so on. But in this chapter, I want to address some of the mechanics–the systems and procedures–that I began putting in place on "the day I became a CEO."

Systems and Procedures: Tools of the CEO's Trade

After realizing that I needed to be a true CEO, not a " business operator" or just a guy running around putting out fires, I faced the question: now what do I do? As so often before, one of my mentors helped me find the way. I described my problems to my friend and mentor Tom. He asked some key questions that made light bulbs go off in my head.

"If I understand what you're saying," Tom remarked, "your company is failing to achieve consistent results. Specifically, you are telling me you have problems in the areas of client identification, client recruitment, and client retention."

"Right," I said.

"So, what systems do you have in place to handle those functions?"

I blinked at Tom like a deer caught in the headlights. I said, "Systems?"

Tom said: "Yes, what are your procedures?"

"Uh...procedures?"

Tom cleared his throat. "I mean, they're spelled out in the manuals, right?"

"Manuals?"

There was a long pause. Finally Tom said: "Jordan, your problems are bigger than you know. But the good news is, there are some proven solutions out there for you."

The very phrase "systems and procedures" sounds intimidating to some people. But relax; it's not rocket science. Most of the work of putting systems and procedures into place and making them work, comes down to common sense. (As usual, that label is not strictly accurate. If these qualities truly were common, fewer companies would fail.)

"Systems and procedures" means:

1. Identify the core functions of your company.
2. Assign each of the core functions to specific people. If your company has more than five employees, create departments.
3. Hire the best people you can find (affordably) to run each department. Don't hire if you have doubts–either about the prospective employee, or about whether you absolutely need more staff!
4. Have your department heads come up with annual and quarterly sub-objectives (in consultation with you) that will contribute to the company's achievement of your overall objective. Have the department heads put these goals in writing. Make sure the goals include *measurable* targets.
5. Give your department heads the authority–and the responsibility–to figure out the best way to meet their individual objectives. Have them create a plan, also in writing, to execute this strategy.
6. Have your department heads and their staffs create employee manuals that define each job–not merely in terms of function, but chiefly in terms of *how the job is expected to contribute to the ongoing responsibilities of the department.* Each employee manual should also spell out precisely how that job is supposed to be performed, step-by-step...as precise as how to turn on the computer and answer the phone. (Yep, that's called "procedures.")

7. Monitor staff to ensure compliance with written procedures and achievement of measurable objectives. Have your department heads train new staff members to understand and follow written procedures.

Now, that wasn't so bad, was it?

The first purpose behind setting up systems and procedures is to make new business happen again and again, consistently; and to make certain that other core functions (such as innovation, customer service, and so on) also achieve measurable objectives consistently. Systems and procedures are a standardized response to identifying recurrent, generic problems.) This standard response is put in place–formalized, routine-ized, and institutionalized–in order to avoid or resolve those problems in the future. Whether you prevent the problems from occurring at all, or just consistently resolve them when they do pop up, either way you reduce them to routine, manageable proportions.

The secondary purpose of setting up systems and procedures is to free up the CEO's time and energy for doing the things that only he can do. They say we elect each President of the United States in order to make just a few big decisions–but they had better be the *right* decisions. Likewise, when a company puts solid systems and procedures in place, the CEO can concentrate on the big picture and making the right decisions, too. That, after all, is his real job.

Now, it's easy to tick off the above list of seven steps, but harder to execute it. Each of the seven steps on that list represents a detailed project in itself. However, you don't have to do it alone. Remember, the CEO's job is to assign these tasks and supervise how they're done, then approve or disapprove the results.

Most of these tasks are ongoing. For example, departmental goals must be continually adjusted, revised and restated as conditions change. But once more, this is mainly the responsibility of your department heads, in consultation with you as CEO. Your prime responsibility in this regard remains one of setting the overall goals and strategy.

Whether it's a CEO and department heads, you by yourself, or you and just one or two employees, additional tools will be required in order to *implement* your systems and procedures. These additional tools may include formal meetings and reports, plus informal intelligence-gathering techniques. (See Chapters 18 and 19 for details.)

From Our Worst Month to Our Best Month...In 30 Days

Adopting a "systems and procedures" approach at my company proved dramatically beneficial–immediately. One month after the zero-revenues crisis that I described at the opening of this chapter, we racked up our biggest month in my company's history to that point.

To my delight, it also became clear that we were creating a positive, self-reinforcing cycle. Becoming more systematic about our jobs, allowed us to grow the numbers. As the numbers grew, we noted what worked, and we became *even more systematic the next time* about precisely duplicating any new actions that seemed to work (incorporating those steps into our existing procedures). And you can bet we wrote it down and kept updating and revising our manuals, too. In this fashion, success feeds on itself.

Taking a more systematic approach to our core business functions also brought a dramatic benefit for me personally. I had reinvented my job. When I took responsibility for setting my company's overall strategy...co-creating systems and procedures with my team...and holding my staff accountable for results...this obviously put more weight on my shoulders.

Yet at the same time, it also liberated me to be the visionary, innovative entrepreneur that I had always wanted to be. I was no longer torn between meddling in my staff's work or letting things drift (with the clear risk that it would all eventually fall apart). My company was running like a well-oiled machine. I am not saying that it ran itself, but my team was running it...smoothly. Like me, they too were taking more responsibility. And, all of us were having more fun.

Not to mention serving our customers better.

And making more money...

Putting the right systems and procedures in place may sound like a dreary matter of paperwork, drudgery, and bureaucracy. *Au contraire:* it is like learning to ride a bicycle or fly an airplane. Once the basic skills become ingrained...once the systems and procedures become organically part of your consciousness (or part of your corporate culture)...you can STOP worrying about falling down or losing your balance, and START focusing on the fun stuff...like, "Where do I want to fly next?"

And the CEO gets to have the most fun of all!

P.S: You Don't Have to Be a CEO to Benefit from Thinking Like One

A department head or a staff member at any level–or for that matter, a sole proprietor–may not be a true CEO. But he can still think like one, and it really pays to do so.

First, think up systems and procedures to streamline your own responsibilities. Even if nobody knows about them but you, you can still significantly increase your productivity this way. Believe me, your superiors will notice the results.

Second, think in a big-picture way about what your responsibilities are to the department or to the company's overall goal. Dream up ways you can creatively and more effectively discharge those responsibilities. Sometimes this may mean becoming a bit of a "job hog," or volunteering for extra duties. If you have increased your own efficiency through adopting good systems and procedures, you will definitely have the time to take on these additional challenges. In a good company, this fact will also be noticed and you'll be marked for raises and promotions.

Finally, dream up ways that your whole department can do more and do better to help the company achieve its goals. These ideas should be carefully thought out, serious suggestions, and they should not be made lightly or routinely. Pass along such suggestions to your superiors. This might be done in a casual remark at the water cooler, or in a formal departmental conference, or even in a company-wide meeting.

The best way to make a suggestion (unless this would be seen as pretentious) is to outline your idea in a written memo to your immediate supervisor…and keep a copy. This puts it on record for all time that you are the person who originally suggested the idea. It also means you can take your time to choose your words with utmost care, and that you won't be interrupted when you try to explain your thoughts. Whether you make your suggestion verbally or in writing will depend on how complex your idea is, and how receptive your superiors have been to employee suggestions in the past.

Even if your idea is ultimately not accepted, in a good company you will receive a reasonable explanation for why not. This means you'll learn something valuable about the company that you didn't know before. At worst, you'll learn a lesson about the realities of corporate politics; at best, you'll learn more about the company's goals and strategies. In a good company, as well, your team spirit in making the suggestion will be noted and *appreciated.*

Do enough thinking and acting "like" a CEO, and someday you may just be one.

Chapter 16:

To Get Your Dream, Build Your Team

From NFL football coaches to high-priced lawyers, from to rock bands to politicians, from military generals to Wall Street financial pros–everybody talks about building a "dream team." Well, it's easy enough to do...if you've got an unlimited checkbook and a high-profile corporate banner to rally around.

(But for most people in the workaday world, building a Dream Team isn't about recruiting half-a-dozen famous superstars in your field. It's a process of finding people who fit YOU and YOUR GOALS and YOUR COMPANY, and who can be trained and encouraged to rise to the occasion. That makes the process of building YOUR Dream Team as individual as a fingerprint.

Whether you're building a brand-new team from scratch, or seeking to transform an existing team, the first step is the same. "To create a Dream Team, find a partner who's unique where you're weak.") I borrowed that line from Mark Victor Hansen, co-author of the *Chicken Soup for the Soul* books. And boy, is it true.

(In every industry on the planet, most successful businesses have a "Mr. Outside" and a "Mr. Inside." Basically, Mr. Outside is the dreamer/visionary, the public face of the company who supplies the big ideas, the enthusiasm, and the leadership. Mr. Inside is the realist behind the scenes, who handles the details and makes the trains run on time.)

(Think Bill Gates (Mr. Outside) and Paul Allen (Mr. Inside).

Or Oprah Winfrey (Ms. Outside) and Jeffrey Jacobs (Mr. Inside). Jacobs is the Harpo Entertainment Group president who structures her business deals and helped Oprah become a billionaire.)

Mark Hansen himself (Mr. Outside) was on his way to conquering the *New York Times* bestseller list, the day he met co-author Jack Canfield (Mr. Inside).

I've always been a Mr. Outside. As a little kid, I began dreaming of doing big things, achieving incredible wealth, fame and fortune. As a company leader, I was and am a big-picture guy, not a detail man.

An earlier chapter of this book mentioned how my company really began to find its footing when I hired my "top lieutenant." She was the company's "Ms. Inside" thanks to her strong abilities to organize, create systems and procedures that get the job done, and bring harmony to the various departments. Somehow, whenever I dream up a big, exciting new venture, she is immediately able to begin translating my vision into concrete steps and plans. Together, we form the core of my company's Dream Team.

The rest of the process of Dream Team-building grows from the same principle that animates the Mr. Outside / Mr. Inside dynamic: namely, the CEO can't do everything. Not only does he lack the time, but he's usually not the best person for most of the jobs around him anyway. As the team leader, it's vitally important to identify what you DON'T do well. What are you NOT good at? The smartest people in this world will admit their businesses have been successful because they find people to perform specialized tasks with great skill.

I certainly know that about myself. I know what I do well: I innovate. But I also know what I don't do well: I'm not a marketing guy, a technical guy, or a paperwork guy. When you come right down to it, I'm really not even a numbers guy! So, what is Jordan Wirsz doing running an investment company? I'm innovative. But I hired people who are really good at numbers, technical issues, and paperwork. I put people in place to do what I don't do well, and I expect them to perform those tasks better than I could. Naturally, when they turn in a stellar performance, I reward them in a way that lets them know I really value their contribution and want them to stay with the company.

As the old saying has it, "The smartest people hire people who are smarter than themselves." You should never fear that hiring strong, capable staff may make you look weak or that your brilliant staff will outshine you. The better your staff looks, the better you look. So a Dream Team begins with a Mr. Outside / Mr. Inside combination, and it continues with a battery of superstars in all the key positions.

Looking for superstars doesn't mean that you should pay top dollar to get the most qualified mail opener you can find. It means that you should recruit someone who has proven ability or who appears to have aptitude for the job; someone whose values and personality are reasonably in synch with your own; and someone who is interested in personal (career) growth–because you're going to set up systems and procedures to translate their quest for personal growth into company growth.

Superstars can be developed, and a good company adopts the mission of doing just that. I want to have the best possible people around me, and I've found a handful of "diamonds in the rough" who, with a little polishing, have done awesome things for my company. They are all superstars in the making.

Teams Work Cooperatively Toward a Common Goal

The CEO's responsibility as a manager is to transform a staff from a group of independent individuals, all pulling in different directions, into an integrated team where everyone is pulling in the same direction. This is accomplished by getting everyone to agree to a common goal and by making them mutually accountable to each other for doing their part to achieve that goal. Even in my own small company, as many as eight people will touch a single deal before it funds. Therefore, in order for my business to function properly, I need those eight individuals to work together as a team.

As for the specifics of how you get everyone pulling in the same direction, there are nearly as many management theories and models as there are companies to practice them. However, many of these theories come down to two basic schools: the top-down, rigidly hierarchal command structure versus the more "collegiate" emphasis on consultation and empowerment. Both schools have their uses, sometimes even within the same company–especially if it's a very large organization.

For example, McDonald's may encourage senior management and department heads to pass along ideas and debate strategy and tactics around the CEO's table every now and then. But the company originally became the leader in its field–in fact, it revolutionized and reinvented its field–by taking its systems and procedures to a level of detail and standardization for each franchisee that was previously undreamed of in the world of fast food.

In general, however, I believe it's a huge mistake to run a business like the old German military–a command structure where "orders flow from the top down, and obedience flows from the bottom up." This model does not encourage people in the hierarchy to think, which means it wastes its most precious resources (brains and creativity). The old German military model also imposes a phony conformity on the organization in the name of "discipline" or "order." That means forgoing the chance to create genuine unity through group participation in the decision-making process. (Please note, I said "participation"–not consensus. More on this in later chapters.)

The greatest companies in the world have blossomed from people thinking, being encouraged to innovate, and staying on the cutting edge of the trends inside and outside of their industry. My own management model, then, is to foster innovation and promote creativity inside my company. This is done by bringing people in and involving them in my decision-making process. I set the overall goals for the company…but when it comes to specific or intermediate goals, overall strategy, and short-term tactics, my team members know they can convince me one way or the other. They can have an impact.

A great deal of valuable innovation has come from our employees who suggest, "Hey, we could do this," or "What if we tried that?" Above all, consultation creates support. When everyone has been consulted, and when everyone feels they have been heard (even if their views are not ultimately adopted), then everyone feels more committed to the goal and more responsible to the rest of the team.

Establishing a common goal helps ensure that team members will not just "interact" with each other in a mechanistic fashion. If every member of the team realizes his or her performance and success depends directly on every other member of the team, they all will cooperate with each other and support each other in the most effective, efficient way.

Suppose there's a supply problem in a small manufacturing company. At first pass, it's much better if the head of manufacturing tells the head of procurement, "Hey, Joe, you promised to deliver 100 pounds of raw materials by the 15th of each month so we can do the subassembly of the widgets. But this month we only got 80 pounds by that deadline. Can you speed it up?" If the problem recurs and procurement is not responsive, manufacturing can buck the issue up the line and management can look into it. But chances are, this won't be needed if the proper team structure and accountability controls are in place.

A Strong Team Is Built On a Strong Foundation

In the worlds of sports, politics, the arts, or business, we hear a lot of talk about team-building, but we rarely hear any discussion of what you're supposed to build the team *on*. A great company builds its team on a strong foundation. A foundation of what?

On a foundation of ETHICS.

If management wants to attract–and *keep*–the best people, managers should say: "These are the people who bring us revenue and protect the longevity of our business. We will honor and respect those people as we would wish to be honored and respected ourselves, if we were in their position."

Yes, we're back to the Golden Rule again: do unto others as you would have them do unto you. But this isn't namby-pamby, dreamy-eyed idealism.

This is hardheaded, pragmatic realism! If you want your people to make an investment in you or your company, you must make an investment in them. Quid pro quo! To me it's just plain common sense to recognize that. As Bill Gates says, "Ninety percent of my company's resources walk out the front doors at six o'clock every night." If you want those resources to walk back in the next morning, then you had better treat your people like gold. They are!"

One of the most successful companies in the Fortune 500 has explicitly written the Golden Rule into its management philosophy and employee training manuals. Cosmetics giant Mary Kay Inc. generates $1.8 billion a year in wholesale revenues–or about $3 billion in retail sales worldwide. Double-digit annual growth has been a Mary Kay staple for years. Approximately 1.3 million independent sales consultants demonstrate Mary Kay products in the U.S. and about 30 other countries. At the peak of the Internet boom, *Interactive Week* magazine ranked Mary Kay in the top five worldwide online retailers.

Maverick Motivator:

Anyone can be a philanthropist! The UCLA's Higher Education Research Institute studied 260,000 college freshmen and found that 66.3 percent of freshmen believe that it is essential or very important to help others. That's the highest percentage to say so in 25 years.

Obviously, this is an aggressive, world-conquering, cutting-edge corporation. Yet the founder of this giant, Mary Kay Ash, built her empire on a people-first ethic. Mary Kay used to tell her top staff that as far as she was concerned, "P&L" meant "people and love." She viewed the company as an extended family, literally. Even after the company grew quite large, she still published an internal company directory that listed all the employees alphabetically by *first name*. She also created the "care list"–a weekly management tool to help her personally telephone every single company employee who was seriously ill, or who had experienced a loss or other family tragedy.

Today, Mary Kay's "people first" tradition is proudly continued by her successors beginning with son and co-founder, chairman Richard Rogers. The care lists are still part of senior management's arsenal.

It's extremely revealing how Mary Kay Inc. won that "top online retailer" distinction. Executives avoided the short-sighted, selfish mentality of: "Hey, thanks to this new technology called the Internet, now we can eliminate the middleman and keep more profits for ourselves!" Instead, Mary Kay management creatively integrated the Internet into their existing corporate structure, further empowering millions of independent field reps.

Most dramatically, Mary Kay Inc. puts its money where its mouth is. (As one successful executive in another industry observed, the boss may say all kinds of nice things to you, and management may say all kinds of nice things about you. But you discover what they really think of you, when they pay you...)

A few years back, Mary Kay Inc. had a (rare) flat year. Naturally, management asked "Why?" A quick investigation revealed that it wasn't the staff's fault: each department had met or exceeded its goals. In fact, across the board, many if not most rank and file members of the Mary Kay team had performed with zeal and excellence, as usual.

Senior management decided to put responsibility for that year's disappointing results squarely where it belonged: on senior management! When year-end bonuses were handed out, vice-presidents, executive vice-presidents, presidents, the CEO and the chairman went empty-handed. Everybody else got the bonuses they had been promised. Chairman Rogers calls it "the May Kay Way" and President David Holl explains: "It's all about the common bond."

Do you think the Mary Kay people went to work the next year, even more enthusiastically determined to show their appreciation and return the loyalty of their bosses? You bet they did!

Enlightened Self-Interest: By Helping You, I Help Myself

The essential insight is, "What's good for you (the employee or the customer) is ultimately good for me (the employer or the company as a whole). By helping you, I help myself."

Raising that insight to the level of principle–and acting upon it consistently–is called "enlightened self-interest."

In the early days of my career, I got very emotional about my company. My feeling was: "It's my creation, my work and blood and sweat and tears, it's my nest egg! I can't give it away...and I won't! I will NEVER give any tiny piece of it away, ever...until I take it public."

Any CEO who hopes to build a significant, market-leading business cannot afford that kind of greed and immaturity. Such attitudes are dead weight and must be thrown overboard immediately, if you want to move fast. Nobody builds a billion-dollar enterprise on his own. From Bill Gates to Walt Disney, they all had help and that help all had a piece of the company. These companies all benefited from key team members who took ownership of their jobs, because they had part ownership of the company.

Today, therefore, I am a strong believer in bonuses, performance-based pay raises, profit sharing, and the like. There are many other places my staff could work–possibly even with better pay or benefits–but I try to provide a fun, rewarding place of employment. I compensate my people competitively, or even above "standard market value" in some cases, because they are valuable, key people. And I try to build employee growth and advancement into the quarterly annual performance reviews and planning.

Making these investments in your employees can help achieve one "precautionary" goal, which is preventing good people from leaving. Even more importantly, it helps achieve a pro-active goal: growing your company. If I can get farther, grow bigger, and move faster by giving my key employees a piece of the action, I am certainly going to do it.

As one self-made millionaire CEO likes to say: "If you find a way to tie employee compensation to departmental productivity or revenues, your employees will lay awake at night, dreaming and scheming about new and better ways to improve the company's bottom line...because they know it will put money in their own pockets."

When you build a team, you're not compiling a collection of assets to exploit, nor an arsenal of equipment or tools to utilize. You're not merely filling out slots on an organization chart, either. You're forging bonds with people...and people are not merely a means to an end. Or at least, they shouldn't be–not even in the corporate world.

People are your partners in success. They may work for you, but they don't belong to you. In many ways, if you're a responsible leader, *you* belong to them.

Always remember: if you want to build a Dream Team, it's YOUR dreams that are invested in its design and growth. So from first to last, YOU must be an integral, intimate part of the team, too.

Chapter 17:

Leadership is About an Endless Line of Goals

Leadership is one of the most romanticized subjects in our society, which means it is one of the topics most surrounded by mythology. We are drowning in clichés about "the lonely burden of power"..."the mysterious nature of charisma"..."the crucial role of strategy"...yadda yadda yadda. Fortunately, there's a healthy corrective. Americans cherish an endless flow of jokes and wisecracks, portraying corporate titans and political giants as fools, crooks, and clowns.

However, this profusion of conflicting ideas and images tells me that most people don't have a clue what leadership really is. So what is it?

U.S. president Harry Truman once offered a humorous yet insightful description of leadership. He claimed that the most powerful leader in the free world is actually "a glorified public relations man who spends his time flattering, kissing and kicking people to get them to do what they are supposed to do anyway." Truman's mocking remark was largely intended as a joke, but on closer inspection it contains a pretty good definition of leadership:

- ¢ He implies the fact that leaders must know how to select the *right goals:* they know which things people are "supposed to do."
- ¢ He includes the fact that *leaders need followers:* simply, "people."
- ¢ Finally, President Truman recognized that in order to attract those people and inspire them to work for those goals, *leaders must use persuasion:* "flattering, kissing and kicking to get them to do" something specific.

Leadership, then, is (1) selecting a goal; (2) convincing others to share that goal; and (3) mobilizing them to work toward the goal. Or in sum: "I see it; you want it; let's go for it!"

Leadership Begins With Vision

A person takes the first step toward leadership when he sees a vision of where people should go. It can be a small vision, as when a kid says to his friends: "Hey, let's go swimming!" Or it can be a large vision, as when a religious figure summons all of humanity to embrace a new system of ethics and theology for all time.

For most of us, our vision will encompass goals that fall somewhere between these two extremes. When Jack Welch took over as CEO of General Electric, he decided that his goal was to make GE the leader in every business that it competed in. In pursuit of that goal, Welch sold off several divisions that he did not believe had the potential to become number one in their sectors—even though they were famous and profitable empires. That's big, bold, visionary action...vastly larger than "Let's go swimming," but considerably less ambitious than "Let's all believe in one God and follow the Ten Commandments."

Like most CEOs, I decide what businesses and markets my company will pursue, and I set the overarching goals for the company to achieve in pursuit of those businesses and markets. For example, I originally decided the company would focus on private money lending in Las Vegas. Under my direction we have begun expanding our market area nationwide. As this book is written, our next measurable overall company goal is to reach a level of success where we're generating a specific dollar figure in monthly net revenues...an amount that is 33% higher than our current average monthly net. Longer-term goals include taking the company public.

Setting annual goals for your company is very much like setting goals for yourself. The goal should be achievable, yet represent a definite challenge. The goal should require everyone to maximize and improve his or her efforts. The goal should be specific and measurable so we'll know if we succeeded or failed, and if so, by how much. The goal should have a deadline attached.

In addition, a goal should be about creating the future, not defending your turf or hanging onto the past. It should be a goal that the CEO and the team feels will help the company forge its own unique identity—not simply to copy somebody else's success, nor to get in line with the latest fad or trend.

A goal should take guts: guts for the leader to proclaim, guts for the followers to agree to attempt. One reason why goal-setting, at its best, is a gutsy activity is because a good goal makes you—and everyone around you—stretch.

Another reason why goal-setting takes guts, is that the best goals are not always the most obvious ones. In fact, the best goals may fly in the face of what customers "say" they want. But great leaders know that customers don't always KNOW what they really, really want...until they see it.

A great leader sees a new product or service in his mind first, long before anyone else has even dreamed of it, and he leads his company to the point where they can offer that product or service to the customer. Sometimes the leader does this despite the fact that his colleagues, competition, and customers are loudly questioning his sanity. Later, after the new idea becomes reality – a successful reality – these former critics either say, "That CEO is a genius" or (more likely) they brag, "I knew all along it would work."

That's why they call it vision!

Setting a goal must imply deciding that certain other potential goals will become a lower priority, postponed, or rejected outright. This implies they will commit the necessary resources of time, money, and attention to achieving the key goal. It also implies having the "stick-to-it-iveness" to deny time, money, and attention to other potential goals. Otherwise, the selection of the original goal is rendered meaningless. Here's the place to beware of the typical, bureaucratic, "play it safe" instinct. When you hear that popular non-battle cry, "Let's do both!" – it is usually a formula for compromise, mediocrity, and perhaps even outright failure.

So, in order to make sure that a key goal really is and remains a key goal, the CEO must have the ability to say "no" at times...and repeatedly. This can be painful. Certain people are sure to be disappointed as a result. But a good leader must have the guts to endure that displeasure. This is why British prime minister Tony Blair once claimed the chief art of leadership is the ability to keep disappointing people!

(By the way, some leaders who want to maintain their popularity with the troops select a chief lieutenant whose job description includes giving subordinates the bad news that their pet projects are being postponed, downsized, or squashed. One such aide famously earned the nickname, "The Abominable NO-Man.")

If my original description of leadership sounded easy, by now it should be clear why leadership is anything but that. True leadership means climbing out on a limb and risking unpopularity in certain quarters.

Communicate Your Vision

Once you're out on the end of that limb, the next step is to look back and say, "Wow, what a great view! You've gotta see this!"

The way you convince others to share your goal – the way you persuade them to become dedicated, enthusiastic followers — is by communicating your vision. Vision is not about telling a story; that is in the past tense. Vision is about painting a picture of the future, showing your team WHERE you want the company to go, and WHAT you want the company to be…

My vision for the future of my company begins with a big building, two or three stories tall, with our name and logo emblazoned on it so they're visible from half a mile away. In the grand entry foyer, I see an imposing reception desk, and on the wall behind the desk is our company logo, mounted on a dazzling chrome backdrop. I see a highly professional yet welcoming receptionist in a well-tailored suit who says, "Hello, sir (or ma'am), how can I help you?"

You walk beyond the lobby to a broad, winding set of stairs. Nearby is a bank of elevators. You ride up, passing two floors that hum with activity. On those floors I see a staff of more than 200 professionals, all dedicated and eager members of the team who are on top of their game and on top of the market. They're making phone calls, making deals, making money, serving a fabulous clientele, and—yes—having a blast while doing all this.

You reach the top floor. The elevator doors roll open smoothly. You are greeted by a cheerful staff person who escorts you down the hall to a huge corner office—my office—with a conference table and an elevated area with a desk. When you walk in, you find me at my computer, reviewing numbers…

On my computer screen I visualize a graphic that pops up with numbers that put us on the *Forbes* list of the fastest-rising companies in America. The screen reveals that my company—now a nationwide organization with branches in every major city from New York to Los Angeles—processed $250 million in business this month, which brought us $30 million in gross revenues. Our monthly net is $12 million.

I see people talking about us around town: that company is so successful! I see CNN reporting: The company has done it again. This time they have funded a glitzy $800 million project in Manhattan.

I see that in my mind as vividly as you dream at night. Those are my dreams, my waking dreams. As the song says, you've got to have a dream if you want to have a dream come true.

Actually, you've got to do more than have the dream; you've got to share the dream and get other people to make it *their* dream, too. When you share those dreams, people modify the details to fit themselves into the picture, and that's exactly what they should do. It means they are co-dreaming with you and they will be co-creating the reality with you, too.

I want my employees to dream: "I could have stock options someday. I could be one of the first 30 employees in a huge company. Maybe we'll open a branch in a bigger city with a thriving market, and Jordan will send me there to run the branch…"

People begin to form that internal aspiration. They should see that goal as vividly as possible, and how it relates to themselves. They should know why they're working so hard on a daily basis, and they should have a reason to work harder...gladly. And sharing your goal, making it public, means everyone on the team can work toward that one purpose.

When I want to share a vision and communicate goals, I don't send a memo. A vision like that is too emotional, too intimate, to be handled so impersonally. A company vision is something to be excited about and to share excitement about. Writing it all down would take you five pages just to set the stage, and then the reader wouldn't get to see the gleam in your eye and catch the enthusiasm in your voice.

At the same time, a company's goal should also be put in writing, along with the overall strategy for achieving it. As with a personal goal, a company goal is not a true goal until it's written down. But this written version is a follow-up record that is given only to the top leadership, and used as a steady reference and reminder for the duration of the timetable that goes with the goal.

In addition to communicating the vision and the goal to the entire team, it's also an excellent idea to keep everyone informed of "how we're doing"—as a company—in terms of reaching our goal. For example, many charitable fundraising operations and political vote-getting operations use the classic wall chart, showing a thermometer with a climbing "temperature gauge" that represents the money or the votes garnered so far. This chart makes a great symbol of the organization's current progress. It's simple, graphic, easy to understand, and it's motivational.

The third component of leadership is mobilizing your followers. This is where classic managerial skills come in, and that subject deserves a chapter to itself!

Chapter 18:

Above All, Leaders Need Followers

Once you've got your team excited about the vision and committed to achieving the goal, it's time to mobilize your forces in pursuit of the goal. This is the basic management function, and there are many valid and useful techniques for accomplishing it.

A few of the basics include management by directive; management by example; management by indirection; management by training; management by walking around; and management by punishment and reward. A good manager uses all of these techniques at different times depending on the situation at hand, the personalities involved, and the time factors of the given situation.

Naturally, every one of these techniques is based on the assumption that you have delegated authority and responsibility to your department heads and their subordinates. Power should be delegated widely, as needed, to give your team the tools they need to achieve their departmental goals. I take a hands-off approach and let people do what they need to do. In fact, I give people enough rope to either hang themselves or to create the world's fastest elevator to success. Good staff members find it exhilarating when someone gives them the authority to make a difference in a company. Bad staff members quickly let you know, through their failure to embrace responsibility, that they don't belong on the team.

Management by directive is simply giving orders: "This is what I want you to do; now go do it." I make sure to do a certain amount of that, partly in order to save time if the requirements are simple and straightforward. Partly I do it to assert my own authority and remind everyone (including me) of who is ultimately in charge. An organization needs somebody at the top who clearly knows what he wants and puts his foot down, driving the group forward. The team likes to know that someone is firmly in charge and confident of his own leadership. So giving outright commands now and then, gives them confidence, too. Confidence can be contagious…and management by directive can be one tool to help spread the contagion.

Management by example is the most powerful technique in the manager's playbook. Some people say it ultimately is the art of leadership in a nutshell. I believe that's an oversimplification, but there is no question that integrity is essential to the most effective leadership. If you want your core values to be respected and emulated by everyone else in the company, then you must "walk the walk, not just talk the talk."

For example, when the boss preaches sermons about giving value to the customer, then cuts corners when fulfilling a major order, the troops get the message that the real priority is shaving a few points off the burn rate – not delivering quality. Worse yet, when the boss sings hymns to company caring and concern for one's colleagues, then acts like his only worry is loss of productivity if a key staffer gets sick, the team gets the message that the company doesn't care about them as people but only as assets.

But when the leadership comes in early and stays late, the rank and file feels good about following suit. When the CEO admits ignorance or apologizes for a mistake, the key staff gets the message that they don't have to pretend to know everything and their own imperfections and shortcomings will be forgiven (within reason).

Management by indirection is a technique that harks back to the lesson that "the art of selling is not to sell." The fundamental tactic here is pretty simple: drop hints and see if your team members pick up on them. Ask questions that subtly plant the answer in the other person's head. I use this one all the time. It's not manipulative; it's a classic technique of Socratic dialog because it is based on the faith that your staff members are smart people who, with a bit of gentle prodding, will come up with the same insights that you did (or if you give them half a chance, they may come up with even better insights). This is the next step in empowering people and delegating authority: encourage them to take that authority and use it creatively.

For example, I went to Rich, our biggest producer, and asked him how we could set up a plan for his succession in case he had a family emergency or got hit by a bus. He said we should probably have somebody cross-trained to handle his job. I agreed that in theory we could do that, but I pointed out this solution would cost a fair amount of revenue to have someone on hand like a fire extinguisher who might never use that cross-training. After all, we don't know if this contingency will every really happen. I said: Say, what about a teaching tool? Maybe we could create a PowerPoint presentation, or…?

Rich said, How about a manual? I said that's a good idea. He said,

"Yeah, but I don't know what to put in a manual." I asked: "Well, Rich, what do you do on a daily basis?" He replied: I come in, talk to investors, do this, do that... I said, "You could put that into your manual, couldn't you?" He lit up, smiled, and said: "Oh, yeah! Sure I could!"

Now, did I feed Rich this idea or did he come up with it himself? I don't know and I don't care. All I know is, Rich offered a suggestion and a workable solution. Now we have a manual that ensures that if Rich is ever off-duty for an extended period, somebody can step in and perform his functions, step by step.

Management by education is the obvious result of creating these employee manuals that I've been talking about. When our company hires a new staff member, we appoint an in-house mentor or trainer who assigns a couple of chapters each week of a 90-day training program. We have progress reviews every 30 days during that program. Afterwards, we have annual performance reviews and employee evaluations. If needed, we encourage every employee to "act like a CEO" by becoming a forward thinker, taking initiative, and considering what else they can do to help grow the company. We encourage them to ask themselves: what part of my job can be transformed into a system or improved service? The purpose is setting a standard and expectation that each team member will want to meet, internally, to become a leader and grow with the company. We want to promote from within, and we want our staff to deserve it.

Management by walking around means don't just stay in your office. Go out and about, look around, and mingle. Eddie Rickenbacker, onetime president of the old Eastern Airlines, used to visit different airports and practice this technique. He would walk through the maintenance crews' work stations and say, "Hi, fellows, what are you doing? How's it going?" He would chat with the mechanics in the grease pits and with the supervisors with the overalls and the clipboards. Then go to the ticketing counter and repeat the process...then the baggage handling department...and so on. He gained endless knowledge about problems, facts, trends, and opportunities from direct observation, long before the department heads caught wind of them. It was also a morale-booster for the front line staff to see that the company CEO cared enough about them and their contribution to visit personally.

My own company is much smaller, of course, so I practice a subtler variation on this technique. Personally, I hate it when people stand over your shoulder and silently stare at your computer screen until you become self-consciously aware of them and ask, "Can I help you?" So I'm very casual about those kinds of oversight questions, and I make sure it never happens in an employee's office or workstation. Instead, I engage them in the break room when I'm getting a cup of coffee, or at the copying machine or in the lunchroom. Then I casually say: "Hey, how's it going? Anything new going on?" I might hear: "No, not much. This payoff on the Jones account just came in." So my questions are very casual, low-key and non-invasive, but I find out what I need to know.

Management by punishment and reward is crucial, but it's an incredibly powerful technique that must be used with great care. Always praise in public, punish in private. You want people to feel good about themselves, and it makes them feel good when you say something positive about them in front of others. We don't hold company-wide meetings often, but when we do I make it a point to go around and praise every single person.

At our last meeting, I said: "Jim, you have done an awesome job of keeping our relationships going with investors that have allowed us to climb out of our rut. Rich, you have come out of nowhere with these investors who funded almost one million dollars last month. Kudos! Lauren, you have worked harder than anyone else in the company. Edgar, you have stepped up the flow, made the extra effort, and that's a big reason why our revenue flow is better. Thank you." And so on.

I make it a point not to leave anyone out. If you praise some and not others, it will create resentment, hurt feelings, or confusion. We follow up with annual, written performance reviews. Raises and bonuses are based on those reviews.

(Telling someone they are not performing up to the company's standards is best done in private, in most cases. On very rare occasions I have done this in public when everyone in the company needs to change his attitude or upgrade her standards. In such times, I may "chop someone's head off" to set an example. This tactic has worked in some ways and failed in others. It does not motivate people or inspire people, but it is a reality check for everyone in the company. If they don't have internal inspiration, and you can't seem to provide external motivation, then you need that reality check.)

My Philosophy of Leadership

Leadership is something you have to work at. It is external and internal. The internal parts are the mulling things over, doing the private meditations and deep soul-searchings that lead to visionary new ideas and directions. The external parts are the cheerleading and coaching that fire up your team and get them behind you as you drive toward making your vision a reality.

My philosophy of leadership is to set high expectations yet give people maximum room for personal growth, expression, and individuality. I want to take the greatest possible advantage of whatever any person has to give, and I recognize that people have different strengths and weaknesses, different quirks and idiosyncrasies, different dreams and desires. For this reason, my company is not a "communist" organization. I don't believe everyone is equal, and I refuse to pretend or expect everyone to be, look, think, or act the same. That is a formula for a boring and stagnant company.

Excitement, growth, and innovation come from flexibility and allowing people to express their personalities. I accept those differences (within the context of professional standards and behavior), and I celebrate that it is our differences that make it possible for various individuals to add different things to the company.

> *"If your actions inspire others to dream more, learn more, do more and become more, you are a leader."*

Chapter 19:

A Good Meeting

Meetings can be exciting, productive, and worthwhile…or they can be boring, obstructive, and a total waste of time. There are three kinds of terrible meetings, and I list them here in ascending order of awfulness:

- The least awful (but still terrible) meeting features the boss reading an entire memo to the staff…a memo that the staff has already read, or has been handed just before the boss reads it out loud. What a bore. If you're going to issue a memo, why read it to people? If you think your staff won't read it or can't understand it, give them a quiz later. Otherwise, respect their intelligence and integrity enough to let them read it for themselves.
- In the second-worst meetings, the boss drones on and on, relishing his captive audience and inflicting the same old anecdotes that his team has probably already heard 100 times before. But nothing gets decided. Or the staff ends up so confused that they return to their jobs and start to tread water, delaying any real action. That's because they're less certain about what direction is the right one, than before the meeting began.
- The absolute worst type of meeting is one where the boss "pretends" to consult his staff, then announces a policy that he'd already decided on beforehand. Sometimes this approach takes the form of asking the staff for their views, then never shutting up long enough to let anyone express an opinion. An even worse variation of this ploy takes the form of encouraging the staff to discuss various alternatives at length, then announcing the pre-determined decision like pulling a rabbit out of a hat. Either way, the pretense of consultation is an insult and a waste of time–yours and the staff's. It's

also deeply corrosive to your relationship with the people who work for you. Believe me, the staff can see right through this charade every time, to the contempt that lies beneath.

I don't even count the type of session where the boss simply screams, rails, and throws a temper tantrum at the staff. That's not a meeting; that's abuse. More than one good employee has been prompted to quit by such a scene, either on the spot or soon thereafter.

To have a good meeting, you must answer three main questions: with whom, what's the agenda, and how often. Above all, be aware of the *purpose* of a good meeting: either (a) to promote discussion so the boss can learn something; or –more rarely–(b) as a motivational tool: to give the CEO a forum to communicate praise or blame in a highly personal way that will have a definite emotional impact on the team.

If you simply need to make a one-way, routine, boss-to-staff announcement, and if you don't require feedback, send a memo or pass along the message verbally through your department heads. Don't waste your time or the staff's time on a meeting just to yak "at" them.

In most good meetings, then, a key purpose is educational. It's an opportunity for the boss to learn something, preparatory to making a decision. Therefore, the CEO announces the meeting agenda up front ("We're looking at launching a new product line, and I want to hear some ideas about whether or not that's a good idea–and if so, how it should be done.") After that, the boss asks a few questions to get the ball rolling, sits back, and mostly *listens*. After all, you don't learn anything new while you're talking. Besides, the more infrequent your comments, the more impact they carry. Follow-up comments by the boss should be for the purpose of guiding further conversation or clarifying what staff members have said.

Sometimes it's important to get a make or break issue on the table because—even if it creates conflict–a lively discussion helps the CEO by clarifying the nature of the various alternatives and their true meaning. When I call a staff meeting, I set the stage for such a productive conflict by asking everyone to express their opinions, no holds barred. I encourage colleagues to argue back and forth a bit. This is not only educational for the boss; it's frequently educational for the team members. For example, you know you're having a productive meeting when the head of R&D says to the director of marketing: "Gee, I didn't realize our new fritzenjammer interface was such a turnoff to so many potential customers. All my tech guys love it, but if you're telling me the average consumer hates it, maybe we should consider a redesign."

As with individual meetings and "management by indirection," I sometimes plant ideas in people's heads during staff meetings. But that's not the same as pretending to consult when you have already made up your mind what to do! Sometimes when you plant an idea, the person considers it then analyzes why that idea won't work, or is inspired to make an even better suggestion. You should stay open to this evolving, organic flow of creativity. Otherwise, as stated, there's no point to consulting people or having a meeting.

To Schedule or Not to Schedule... It Depends On Your Purpose

When the legendary Lee Iacocca took over Ford Motor Company (before he went to Chrysler and performed miracles there), he began to develop a strategy for meetings that turned into a powerful management tool: a quarterly review system. He met one on one with every senior executive, every three months. The agenda for these meetings was simple yet straightforward, Iacocca explains.

"I've regularly asked my key people–and I've had them ask their key people–a few basic questions: 'What are your objectives for the next 90 days? What are your plans, your priorities, your hopes? And how do you intend to go about achieving them?'" Iacocca said this system not only holds the senior executives accountable to the CEO, it makes employees accountable to themselves.

At my company, our meeting schedule is a little different, but the sense of structure and purpose is much the same. I take the company's financial temperature every day. I get weekly reports from department heads; every month we meet and go over them. Meetings with the entire company are scheduled on an as-needed basis. I find if you schedule them on a fixed calendar, many meetings will happen when there is no issue that needs to be addressed.

Timing of meetings is an important factor, too. I believe people are not fully awake at the beginning of the day and are tired by the end of the day. My own acuteness peaks at 11AM, so I schedule meetings for 10:30 or 11AM until 12:30 or 1PM. Experience shows that our best, most insightful meetings happen in that zone.

Unifying Staff Behind the CEO's Decisions

If one primary purpose of a good meeting is to educate the CEO (and to let staff members educate each other), a second key purpose is to forge a group commitment to whatever decision emerges. To this end, it's important to let everyone feel they have made a contribution to the discussion of a new action plan or the resolution to a problem. When team members feel their input has been heard and considered, even if it ultimately isn't used, they feel invested in a plan. When they feel invested in a plan that they've worked out together—a plan they will be collectively responsible for—that feeling creates teamwork and vastly increases the odds that the new plan will succeed.

If some staff members don't speak up during these consultative meetings, I call on them. "Jane, what would you do?" Everyone should be heard from, without exception.

Again, this is not a pretense of consultation; it should be the real thing. Sometimes, the person who has hung back and said the least, actually makes the most surprising and useful contribution to the discussion—if and when they are prompted to speak up. Often, the very reason they were silent before is because they were afraid to drop a bombshell on the group (and the boss). Staying open to staff input—even last-minute, reluctant input–is an excellent way to ensure that decisions are based on the greatest possible knowledge base.

And by the way, when somebody does drop a bombshell, don't chew them out. Be sure to thank them profusely!

Not all meetings do or should result in an immediate decision. Sometimes the best conclusion is for the leader to say: "Okay, I've heard some useful ideas here and you've all given me some good stuff to think about. I'll take all of this under advisement and will let you know what our next step is. In the meantime thanks for your input, everybody." The next step may be a follow-up meeting to consider a new development or a fresh angle on the issue. Or it could be a memo or verbal announcement of a new policy or initiative.

The most productive meetings *do result in a clear decision* or firm commitment to a new policy, then and there, before everyone gets up from the table. In this case, the meeting might end with the CEO making a statement such as:

"Based on what I've heard here today, it seems clear that we need to drop the Alpha approach to customer service and concentrate on the Beta approach. So, that's what we're going to do. Department heads, please work up a plan for how your group can take specific steps to get the ball rolling on this...I'd like that document on my desk by Monday. Thanks for your contributions, everyone, and I know I can count on all of you to do everything possible to make this new policy succeed."

IMPORTANT: It is not necessary or desirable that the group achieve 100% consensus behind a policy. In fact, some of the brightest business leaders strongly distrust such consensus and see it as a sign that some "buried land mines" have yet to be unearthed, and could blow up in their faces if they go forward with a certain policy.

Alfred P. Sloan, the genius who built General Motors into America's biggest company in the mid-20th century, supposedly once ended a meeting on this surprising note: "Well, fellows, it seems we're all in complete agreement on the decision. In that case, I'm going to put off talking about this subject any more until our next meeting. Let's give ourselves time to work up some healthy disagreement. Maybe then we can argue our way to a better understanding of what this issue is really about."

That other automotive wizard, Lee Iacocca, also held a low opinion of management by consensus. Waiting for 100% agreement on everything, he said, is slow...results in cautious, bland actions...prevents real accountability and flexibility...and besides, he added, it takes all the fun out of running a company.

Ultimately, the CEO has the responsibility for every plan, and he should be the one who makes the final decision–over opposition if necessary. Good leaders relish this power, and they exercise it with flair.

Perhaps the most famous example of this was the time President Abraham Lincoln had a cabinet meeting where he asked the Secretary of State, Secretary of War, and so on for a vote on a certain proposal. When Lincoln asked for the "Nays," every single member of his Cabinet raised his hand in opposition.

Then Lincoln asked for the "Ayes." He raised his own hand–alone, with no supporters.

Lincoln said: "Very well. The ayes have it."

Meetings as Motivational Tools

The title of this chapter asserts that a good meeting is one where the boss talks least. Nine times out of ten, that's true. But the tenth time is a motivational meeting, and that's one where the boss talks most. In fact, he may be the only one who speaks at all.

Since I have made such a big deal out of the difference between motivation (external) and inspiration (internal), let me repeat here that each worker should be responsible for his or her own continuing inspiration and inner drive. But the leader can and should provide a judicious amount of external motivation now and then: the classic prods to get the team moving toward the goal. As previously discussed, these include sharing the vision, communicating the goal itself, and offering carrots and sticks...incentives and disincentives...praise and rewards...censure and (if necessary) demotions, fines, or firings...to mobilize the team into constructive, consistent action.

Meetings can be an excellent place to do some of these things. But remember, if you're going to hold a motivational meeting, you need to prepare your speech in advance. Make sure your purpose is clear–and remember, you're basically there to instill an emotion at this point, either positive or negative.

For example, one purpose for a motivational meeting might be for the boss to share his vision of the company's future and to get the team excited about playing an active part in realizing it.

Another purpose could be simply to say "Thank you," praise each team member for his or her outstanding contributions, and perhaps even hand out bonuses.

Yet another type of motivational meeting might have the purpose of putting the fear of God into the team. For example, suppose productivity is down and investigation reveals the staff has not been meeting its obligations. The boss calls a meeting and announces: "We have a serious problem. Productivity rates have fallen 23%, on-time performance is down 31% and cash flow is down 50%. If anybody here doesn't understand what his or her job is, now is the time to speak up. I or your direct supervisor will be happy to enlighten you. But most of us do understand our jobs; we're simply not doing them. Ladies and gentlemen, we're going to walk out of here and get back to work immediately. We're going to bear down and get the job done. We're going to bring those numbers back up to the high 90s in the next two weeks, or else I promise you, heads will roll. That means not everybody who is in this room (or around this table) today will be here next time."

Then dismiss the group. No conversation, no backtalk, no commentary. When you have to deliver bad news, keep it short and to the point. That is a tough meeting to have, but sometimes you have to deliver this type of message. Such an ultimatum should only be delivered when all the other, more positive motivational and managerial techniques have failed, of course.

The good news is, this kind of measured "reality check" almost always gets results. Studies have shown that most people are more jolted into immediate action by the desire to protect what they have, than by the desire to create or gain something more. At the same time, keep in mind that "management by ultimatum" is not a productive long-term tool. Done once, it's electrifying. Done repeatedly, it's dispiriting. Accordingly, it should only be used in real emergencies.

When it's Time to Fire Someone

In the first 18 months of building one of my companies, I had to let a lot of people go. At times, it seemed we might need a revolving door for all the people who were coming and going so quickly. Making the decision to fire someone is never easy–but if the company is suffering, if we are losing more than we're gaining from that person's presence, then we're going backwards and it's the clear responsibility of the boss to let the non-productive person go. You owe it to yourself, you owe it to the company, and you owe it to the rest of the staff, who should not be expected to pull the weight for a deadbeat.

Before firing a problem employee, give him or her verbal warnings in a series of private, sitdown, one-on-one meetings. If the problem is a need for more training or closer supervision, provide it. But if the problem is a personal issue–including substance abuse–be frank about the fact that the company cannot accept this issue impinging on the employee's performance. And of course, express concern for the person's health and offer to be as supportive as possible as they tackle their issue...Whatever it may be.

In any case, be sure to keep written records of these verbal warnings. Follow up with brief, written memos to the person, confirming what was discussed. Keep copies of those memos in the employee's file. This creates a paper trail that can help prevent a wrongful termination lawsuit later, if it's necessary to terminate their employment.

If this series of warnings and offers of assistance fails, let the person go.

To fire someone, I wait until Friday and ask the person to stay a few minutes late. We sit down and I review the positive things about their record. I remind them that we're an aggressive, hyper-growth-oriented company, and explain that I don't see us moving in the same direction. I say: "Zeke, as things are developing you are not going to be able to meet the demands I am going to put on you. I don't want you to feel like you're doing a bad job. I don't want to resent the fact that you're not performing to my expectations. I think you'll do a great job for someone else but I'm sorry, I can't have you here any longer. It's just not a good fit."

Never allow the person to rationalize or make excuses for their poor performance. When someone is given the opportunity to rationalize, they'll have all kinds of reasons why it wasn't their fault. If you permit them to make you feel guilty, or talk you into keeping them on against your better judgment, you're not a strong person and you have only made the situation worse.

So if the person starts to make an argument, say: "I'm sorry, but the decision has been made." Then stand up and say, "You'll need to give me your key and clean out your desk. Take your time. I'll have your severance check for you when you're ready." Let them clean out their desk, then trade the check for the key, wish them well, and usher them out the door.

Handling firings this way may seem blunt. But a brisk, no-nonsense approach of straightforward "honesty without blame" is actually the kindest possible way of handling a dismissal. Holding such meetings after hours on a Friday minimizes any disruption to the company's normal routine. On

Monday morning, the only change is that person doesn't show up. Don't make a mystery about it to the staff; tell people simply and briefly that so-and-so is no longer with us. This can be done verbally or in a memo.

Sign of a Great Meeting: FUN!

I have saved the best news about meetings for last. A GREAT meeting is not only productive–it's fun, because it's an exercise in group dynamics, brainstorming, and creativity. There definitely are times when two heads are better than one, and eight are better than two. A great meeting is also galvanizing because people leave with a clear sense of possibilities and purpose, a feeling that they have been challenged to do something important, and appreciation for the fact that they are being allowed to make a significant contribution to an exciting project.

The most creative, collaborative process emerges when everyone is encouraged to contribute. To foster this, you should set ground rules that any and every idea will be heard and written on the blackboard (or whatever), without —at first–being criticized. Try to list as many ideas as possible, no matter how off-the-wall or impossible they may seem at first glance.

In a surprising number of cases, a suggestion that originally seemed foolish or unattainable at first glance, can later be viewed from a new perspective that suddenly makes it appear totally do-able and desirable. Letting ideas sit and "percolate" in people's minds for a while, without passing judgment pro or con, facilitates this shift in perspective.

After a good hour of such brainstorming, the leader can shift the agenda from ideas to analysis. Again, set some ground rules. Don't allow anyone to say, "You're wrong" or "That's a bad idea because..." Instead, require team members to couch their comments in terms that acknowledge the subjectivity of all opinions, such as: "That concept doesn't work for me because..."

Offer a plausible-sounding (but flawed) idea of your own, and accept it gracefully when team members shoot it down. When the team sees that the boss can take criticism without losing face–and that he can even voice sincere appreciation for corrections–they will be more ready to check their own egos at the door in service of productive give-and-take. (Manipulation? No, management by example!)

When meetings are run along these lines, they can actually take on the best aspects of a game. There is structure, but freedom within that structure to be a little bit playful. If you hold enough meetings in this spirit, your team members will actually come to look forward to them.

Imagine that!

Phase 3:

BUILD Your Wealth

my Maverick 5 Moment

After I got my pilot's license, I figured I would take the next step and go for my instrument rating.

As a regular pilot, you're always looking out the window to see what's happening. In instrument flying, the presumption is that you're flying in fog, or at night, or in a storm, with zero visibility.

Many non-pilots don't realize it, but when you're in the air and can't see anything, it's frighteningly easy to get turned around, to assume a crazy angle to the ground, or even be flying upside-down. You just don't have the normal sights to tell you what's happening.

So when on instrument approach, you're looking at those gauges and your life depends on whether or not you can correctly interpret and extrapolate a lot of different information from many different places. If some of your instruments fail...well, you have to struggle to get information from sources other than the ones that you just lost.

This is a very difficult task–it's probably the hardest rating I've earned. Can you imagine what it feels like to steer a plane in for a landing based on just one or two abstractions: a little gyro that shows you a directional heading, and an altimeter that tells you how close the ground is coming?

But that's reality. Life-or-death decisions must be made every day based on less than perfect information. Elaborate plans must be revised quickly or abandoned as conditions change around you like swirling clouds in a violent sky.

In the final analysis, you simply have to decide, "I'm going to do this." You bring the plane in...

Chapter 20:

Everything in Life is a Risk

(The Biggest Risk of all is Doing Nothing)

We live in a risk-reward economy. Those who take risks and succeed, are rewarded. The bigger the risk, the bigger the reward. All the gain I've ever seen has come out of taking risk. Every CEO or president of any large company that I've ever spoken to says exactly the same thing: you grow by taking risks.

If you're starting a business, launching a political campaign, or aiming to break the world record in speed skating, you are taking a risk that your investment of time, energy, and money may not pay off as hoped. But if your investment does pay off, the reward is big—and life is sweet.

This is where courage comes in. Courage is the ability to take action when you know there is risk involved. Like inspiration, courage comes from the heart (in fact, the very word "courage" comes from the French, *le Coeur*–the heart).

Inspiration tells you: "I need to do this; I'll be so happy when I do this; here are the results that I want to achieve. This is why I'm going to do it." Courage tells you: "And damn it, I am GOING to do it!"

My successes have come when I've taken risks—when I have been willing to move beyond my own comfort levels and the comfort levels of those around me. Every goal I've achieved in life, everything I've done that I'm proud of, came out of taking a risk. I have led my own company to places where everyone in the company says (when I announce the goal): "Are you out of your mind? What are you doing?"

And I'm proud to say we've been really successful at it. Some people now look at me as a hero because I'm the guy who said, "I believe we can make this happen, and it is what is going to happen"—and we went and did it. Well, I'm no hero but I am somebody who understands, as Andre Gide once said, that "One doesn't discover new lands without consenting to lose sight of the shore for a very long time."

Just Because It "Feels" Risky, Doesn't Mean It Is a Genuine Risk

What determines the size of a risk is what you have to lose–not how emotionally uncomfortable you are with the potential outcome. Judging solely by emotion, the biggest risk I ever took was quitting my professional pilot's job in Florida, moving to Vegas, and beginning my new career. I felt deep turmoil over this action because my emotions kept telling me: "I've put all this time and money into getting flight training and certifications, but now that I have a position in the industry, I'm leaving it. I'm going into an industry I don't know."

Again and again, I asked myself: "What in the world am I doing?" (Several friends and colleagues asked me the same question.)

So I talked to my mentor George about it. I said, "I am really stressing over all this risk."

He said: "What risk? You know how to succeed in business. You have already run a couple of successful businesses, right?"

"Maybe, but I don't know how the mortgage lending industry works."

He asked, "Jordan, how old are you?"

"I just turned 19."

"You must be kidding me with the idea that you're taking a big risk," he said. "You're not married. You don't have kids. You don't own a house. You haven't invested years into a job and a retirement pension. You could become a multimillionaire five times and go bankrupt five times before you get married. What risk are you taking?"

"Well…I could lose the $7,000 in my savings account. And I'm giving up my job in aviation."

George scoffed at this. "So what? You've still got your commercial pilot's license; you've still got flight hours. If necessary, after a year you can get back into that field."

"Yeah…I guess that's sorta true," I mumbled.

"Jordan, it's not 'sort of true.' It's overwhelmingly self-evident. You're crazy for thinking you have to hang onto anything. You're 19 years old! If you lose everything, it's okay. If you fall on your face, you can still rebuild and become a multimillionaire before you're 25. In fact, you can fall on your face 10 years from now and still retire a multimillionaire. What is the big deal?"

I looked at George and said: "You know, you're absolutely right. Now is the time in my life that I can afford to take that risk." I didn't have a marriage, a mortgage, a house or even a dog. I had little to lose, so by definition I was not taking a big risk.

Taking a Risk vs. Taking a Chance

Everyone has to take risks. Starting a business is a risk...hiring a person is a risk...changing a procedure is a risk...adopting a new goal is a risk. The CEO's job is to take an educated risk, and to ensure that no unnecessary risks are taken. Martha Stewart puts it this way: "Take risks, not chances."

The difference between a risk and a chance is information and assessment.

An *educated* risk is the antidote to chance-taking. So gather plenty of information about the possibilities, the pros and cons, before you take a risk. Notice, this does not mean learning everything there is to know about a situation. That's an impossible demand, and in practice it becomes an excuse for delay and inaction.

Beyond gathering facts, seek out informed opinion. This is where a network of experienced peers and mentors is invaluable. But, beware of the fact that when a major potential risk is involved, advisors tend to become cautious. Understandably, they don't want to be blamed if everything goes wrong. So listen to informed opinion, but don't be ruled by it.

An assessment of risk needs to include a frank appraisal of the downside. When you see a risk with a reward that looks worth taking, yet has a serious potential downside, you may be well advised to try to hedge in some way. Mitigate the risk as much as possible. You can sacrifice by giving yourself a financial cushion: sell your home, get a cheaper car, put some money in the bank. If you don't have all that much in the way of assets to begin with, then you are not risking much.

Hedging your bets does NOT mean always splitting the difference and ordering some from Column A and some from Column B. Life is not a Chinese restaurant! Hedging means having a reserve contingency or a backup plan. But these should not interfere with full commitment, once you decide to go forward with a well-considered risk. As the old saying has it, you cannot leap a 20-foot chasm in two 10-foot leaps. It's all or nothing!

Coping With Worry and Anxiety

People want certainty about what the future holds. That's understandable and to a point, prudent. At the same time, this desire cannot be allowed to overrule our capacity to take risks. The trick is learning to live with a degree of uncertainty.

The two big psychological barriers to healthy risk-taking are worry and anxiety. Worry is a specific fear that a specific negative outcome will occur; anxiety is a vague, overhanging dread that "somehow" everything is "just going to go wrong." Worry has some basis in rationality; anxiety is a psychological condition that says more about the person's inner state than about the objective situation. Worry means concentrating on the negative, and that in itself tends to bring about a negative result. Anxiety means existential dread, and it ruins your ability to enjoy life–even if the risk is carried off with fabulous success.)

Worry and anxiety are the killers of opportunity. If you're feeling worried or anxious, then you are putting yourself under stress. You are frazzled. The quality of your efforts will reflect those emotions and that mindset. If you're too busy looking over your shoulder at the big disaster that you are afraid is gaining on you, you are not looking ahead.

(It's like that cliché shot in half of the horror movies ever produced by Hollywood. The good guys are running away from the Horrible Monster, but they spend so much time looking back as they run, they trip and fall…putting themselves in easy reach of the Horrible Monster.)

Focusing on potential disaster in business is very similar: it means if you spend all your time focusing on danger, you cannot perceive where safety lies. In this case, safety lies in the possibilities and options that might make the venture successful. Such lack of vision, in turn, affects the outcome of the opportunity. It also impacts how people perceive you and your company, and reduces your odds of being offered additional opportunities in the future. (People are attracted by confidence and they are put off by lack of confidence.)

Education, as we said before, is the preventative against chance-taking, and it's a huge part of the antidote that can overcome negative emotions of worry and anxiety. If you have done your due diligence…if you have studied the market and the facts of the case…if you have consulted your team, your peers, and your colleagues…then make your best judgment and rest on the fact that you have done your best. That's all anyone can do.

The sign on the CEO's desk says "The Buck Stops Here" because all the easier decisions can be made at lower levels of the organization. The tough decisions, by definition, are ones where you can only get a 75-25, or 60-40, or even 55-45 odds of success. But if that's the best you can do, it's the best you can do.

To return to Martha Stewart, she says she ran her greatest risk when she borrowed $85 million to buy *Martha Stewart Living* magazine from Time-Warner. As with any wise CEO, she asked herself–and her team–all the daunting "what if?" questions. What if all the talented people who put the publication together should leave? What if lifestyle magazines go out of style? What if the Stewart brand gets overexposed?

But Martha calmed those fears with knowledge. She knew her market, and herself. She predicted (correctly) that the home and lifestyle sector was on the verge of a historic boom. She knew how to build and retain a great staff. And she realized that far from risking overexposure, acquiring the magazine was a crucial step in solidifying her brand identity.

(By the way, Oprah Winfrey later did likewise with her magazine. She and her team probably studied the same basic dangers and came to the same basic conclusions. If anything, Oprah had more reasons to worry about overexposure and market downturns. But like *Martha Stewart Living, O–The Oprah Magazine* has also proved stupendously successful.)

Another antidote to worry and anxiety is willingness to accept the possibility of loss in advance. When you assess the balance of risk and reward in a given opportunity, and it creates mainly worry or anxiety, it means you cannot accept the possibility of loss. So, don't pursue that opportunity. Don't gamble with anything that you feel you cannot afford to lose.

If there is enough excitement from a potential opportunity, if there is likely possibility of success that makes this risk so much more attractive than what you're doing, and the risk-reward balance is there, that is a move you make. Then, even if you lose, you will able to say: "Okay, I lost that one, but it was a good effort and a smart play. I learned something from this and I'll be smarter about things when I try something of this sort, the next time."

The Risk of Doing Nothing

There are times when "wait and see" is actually the right move, but those times are becoming scarce. I will say this: those who elevate risk-avoidance and decision-avoidance to the level of prime values, guarantee that they will eventually turn into a fossil. (A fossil–that's an ancient artifact that may have been around for a long time, but which shows absolutely zero signs of life.)

A good leader is biased in favor of action, period. He or she recognizes that even in the midst of uncertainty, doing nothing is often the greatest risk of all. Failing to act allows small problems to grow into big problems. An excessive focus on avoiding all possible risk, invites the competition to take the lead. It means being passive and letting circumstances dictate your fate, instead of being active and taking charge of your own destiny. A habitual refusal to act, breeds fear and anxiety, which makes it even harder to act the next time. Determination to act, when carried through, makes it easier to act the next time.

Nobody has summed up this attitude better than Helen Keller: "Security is mostly a superstition. It does not exist in nature, nor do the children of men as a whole experience it. Avoiding danger is no safer in the long run than outright exposure. Life is either a daring adventure–or nothing."

Chapter 21:

Before the Battle, Plans Are Everything

This chapter is about setting your big-picture strategy, and about having the flexibility to change your tactics as circumstances dictate. Both are crucial to your success.

First, for just a moment, I'm going to talk about D-Day, the successful Allied invasion of France during World War II. Why bring up this bit of history in a book about modern success strategies? Because the strategic lesson of D-Day is *spectacularly* applicable to business today. This lesson also applies to any long-term effort, for that matter. (The headline of this chapter comes from a remark made by Dwight Eisenhower, the Supreme Allied Commander in World War II, who largely planned the D-Day invasion.)

On D-Day itself, certain Allied forces landed on the wrong beaches, often with the wrong equipment. In these circumstances, detailed plans didn't help. Advance planning was of no use when leaders were separated from their men. All the blueprints in the world couldn't solve the problem when "floating" tanks and bulldozers rolled off the landing craft and sank like stones into the rough seas of the Atlantic Ocean.

Despite all this confusion, Allied troops rallied and won the battle. They won because they had been trained to take the initiative and to improvise.

The defending Nazis lost the battle because they had been trained to wait for orders–and in this case, the right orders never came. Coastal defenses had been set up on the assumption that a certain kind of attack would materialize at a certain time and place. When that attack failed to happen as expected, and where expected, the Nazis' rigid command structure left no room to maneuver.

Their plans were worthless. But they refused to change them, so they lost.

It doesn't take much imagination to see that this lesson absolutely applies to business and personal growth!

**Goals tell you where you're going.
Strategy tells you how to get there.**

Former GE chairman Jack Welch has a favorite motto on this subject. He says: "Strategy is not a lengthy action plan. It is the evolution of a central idea through continually changing circumstances."

Notice, Welch begins with one fundamental assumption: circumstances WILL change. And they will change continually! You can depend upon it.

It's up to us how to react to those changes. We can dig in our heels, shut our eyes, and bull forward with the same plan–allowing no alterations or fresh thinking. Or, we can be prepared to improvise, adjust, and "flex our flexibility." Obviously, the latter option is the one Welch (and every other wise leader) recommends. For this reason, a good strategic plan is not carved in stone but written in pencil–and there's usually an eraser somewhere handy nearby!

To create a strategy, begin by asking the basic questions that define every goal in life, in business or long-term campaign. The people at Leadership Strategies Inc. (Atlanta, GA) have broken down the key questions that should be asked into four common-sense groupings:

1) Where Are We Now?

Questions in this group include: what do our potential customers want? Who are our competitors? What are the key conditions in our market? What are the key trends in our industry? What resources and needs do we have, ourselves? What are our strengths and weaknesses?

2) Where Do We Want To Go?

Questions in this group include: What is my vision? What is our mission statement? When I translate our vision and mission into a concrete, overall goal, what does it look like? What specifics does it entail? What preliminary goals and subsidiary goals are part of the overall goal?

3) How Will We Get There?

Questions in this group include: How can my team leaders and I break the overall goal down to specific, achievable steps (sub-goals)? What are the guiding principles that team members should refer to, as they pursue their objectives? What are the basic methods or activities we will use? What will be our working tools? Should we expand the team? What obstacles stand in our way? How will we overcome, bypass, or transcend them? What are our priorities–what will we focus on first? Which issues will we delay for now?

In a business environment, these questions may also include: Who are our customers and how will we find them? How will we attract them? How will we land deals with them or make sales to them? How will we service them?

4) How Will We Monitor Our Progress?

Questions in this group include: What systems and procedures will we use? What measurable benchmarks (and methods of measurement) will be included in our annual, quarterly, and monthly objectives? How will management review performance, with whom, in what setting, and how often?

To these four categories, I would add a fifth:

5) How Will We Adjust Our Tactics In Midstream?

Questions in this group would include: what is the failsafe or trigger point, beyond which we know that major tactical changes in methods and procedures should be adopted? How will we know when it's time to change our basic objectives and sub-objectives on each level–individual, departmental, company-wide? How will we go about defining and executing those changes? Do we have the beginnings of a fallback plan or alternative strategy in mind?

My Company's Central Idea

What follows are excerpts from my original business plan for my company, the basic strategic document that guided my creation of the company. I reproduce it here, exactly as it was first written, in all its flaws and limitations.

The reason for showing you this document is not because it's the greatest business plan in the world–but because it's a relatively simple, straightforward example of a strategy that worked. However, a big part of the reason it worked is because we change the company every time events or circumstances warrant it! (Today, in fact, the nature of my company is almost nothing like the description set forth in this original plan. It evolved as all successful businesses do.)

Note that the core idea of the company is summed up in a 46-word mission statement at the very beginning of the document. Jay Conrad Levinson of *Guerilla Marketing* fame suggests that for communications purposes, every company should be able to sum up its core concept and appeal in seven highly-charged or super-symbolic words–if not fewer than seven. Actually, that's a pretty good exercise for CEOs to perform internally, simply to make sure they are crystal-clear on their core idea. With just seven words, there's not a lot of room for vagueness or having it both ways.

For example, Microsoft's slogan is exactly seven words: "Where do YOU want to go today?" But these words are pregnant with meaning. *To me, they imply a customer-driven company that focuses on empowering the con-*

sumer and assisting people to create and realize their own agendas, explore their potential, and realize their dreams–whether it's using the company's software, surfing the Internet with the company's help, or playing one of the company's video games.

There–I just summed up the core idea of Microsoft in 42 words, extrapolated from their slogan.

Diamond Bay Investments Inc.
Business Plan, effective (Month/Date/Year)

Company Mission Statement

Diamond Bay Investments is committed to maintaining, growing, and creating financial wealth for its investors. With clear intension and direction, the company plans for the financial future of its partners. It creates stability, security, and hassle free real estate trust deed loan investments.

Keys to Success

The key to the company's success is to treat the investor's capital as our own. In order to maintain investors, we must diligently place their money into quality trust deeds in a reasonable amount of time in order to maximize the investor's rate of return. Being honest with investors, borrowers, and employees alike, coupled with integrity and diplomacy will bring a powerful and positive reputation to the company.

In addition to operating with the highest level of honesty and integrity, it is equally important to obtain, and maintain relationships with investors, sufficient enough to fund a minimum of $XX million each year. Additionally, finding the quality and quantity of loans to place those funds hold a large part of the success process.

Company Ownership

(Company name) Inc. is and will continue to be a solely owned subchapter "S" corporation. Employees with profit sharing capability will be implemented when the profits and performance supports the value for that purpose.

Company Vision

The company will become the largest and most prestigious Private Money lending institution in the U.S. Through honesty and integrity in our business dealings; we will grow at a stable and significantly fast rate. Each member of the Diamond Bay team will work diligently to increase production, minimize risk, and maximize profit for the company.

The company will always put the investors first. It will be the NUMBER ONE priority to put customer service and company reliability at the top of our list. The company will always act in the best interests of its investors, protecting, and securing investments, which are adequate to the risk and return standards of each individual client.

Divisions & Key Staff

Several divisions of the company will begin to take shape. These divisions include:

1. Institutional Lending for both residential and commercial
2. Property acquisition, management, and sales
3. Loan servicing and foreclosure dealings

The start of the company will consist of the following entities:

1. President Jordan Wirsz: this position will initially start as building and maintaining relationships with investors and borrower oriented networks, as well as underwriting and examining loans, and representing these loans to each investor.

2. Account Executive/Marketing Rep. (person's name here): this position will be to market mortgage and real estate companies for potential Private Money loans. This will include creating an awareness of the company's Private Money products, networking for referrals, and maintaining a substantial amount of marketing materials such as flyers. This position will also include the duties of setting up key meetings with mortgage companies and their staff (including management, Loan Officers, and other employees) to create an awareness of our Private Money products.)

3. Administrative assistant and office manager: this position will entail phone duties, office supplies and appliance management and coordination, personal assistance to President, initial Doc preparation, title coordination, accounting/book keeping, marketing material coordination and ordering, and state/federal compliance.

As the company grows, the following entities will be added to the team:

1. Marketing Department
2. Investor Relations Department
3. Closing & Coordination Department
4. Underwriting Consultants
5. Accounting Department
6. Loan Servicing & Foreclosure Department

Headquarters & Office Space

The company's corporate headquarters will be located in Las Vegas, Nevada. Further expansion will include branch offices in California, Arizona, and Florida for local lending presence. The company will own its own commercial building, worth no less than $X Million. At least 50% of the office space will be used to house our administrative network, with the remainder of space being leased out.

Marketing

The marketing department will implement the strategy that will include the following:

Referral networking, including educating team members about how to get referrals, and implementing strategy to obtain referrals from current and past clients.

Account Executives and Loan Officers for originating loans. The account executives will work closely with various mortgage and real estate companies to create an awareness of the company and its products/services, and will solicit loans on a daily basis. The Loan Officers will create an inflow of institutional business, which will in turn generate Private Money business, and further expand the presence of the company.

Postal Mailers, which will include direct mail pieces to solicit investors, as well as to market seminars regarding Private Money Investments

Investment strategy seminar hosting to create a database of investors willing to lend their money in trust deeds through the company

Web presence, which will include loan soliciting, as well as investor soliciting. Our web presence will also be that of an informational aspect, to create a better feel for potential clients

Radio/Television advertising, including marketing for seminars, and direct solicitation for both investor call-ins, and name recognition.

Foreign investor market analysis, marketing plans, and execution.

Sales Strategy & Objectives

The sales strategy is based on ease of obtaining a loan, little to no underwriting guidelines and qualifications to meet, and time needed to close. Most institutional lenders can make or break a loan based on small intricacies, which would not affect Private Money in any way. Because credit ratings and history is not a factor involved in the Private Money decision process, qualifications are fast & easy, strictly based on the equity strength and salability of the property.

The Sales Objectives for (first year of operation) is as follows:

This paragraph, which is not reproduced here, established an overall corporate goal as a specific dollar figure, which was broken down into two types of specific loans, giving their average size and interest rate with return period and net that would accrue to DBI; plus property investments giving average profits per unit and total contribution to the bottom line.

The other paragraphs spell out the goals and objectives for specific departments including Investor Relations; Closing and Coordination; Underwriting; Accounting; Loan Servicing And Foreclosure; and Service Business Analysis.

Additional sections outlined my Competition Analysis; Company Goals & Financial Critical Objectives; Investor Critical Objectives; the Financial Plan (including basic assumptions, projected expenses, break-even point, projected P&L, and projected cash flow.

Conclusion

Based on the information within this plan, the company will succeed with a positive cash flow in its first fiscal year in business. All market indicators and previous efforts and experiences have shown a positive outlook on the future of the company.

And then I signed it: Jordan Wirsz, President.)

The EVOLUTION of a Central Idea

Remember Jack Welch's definition of good strategy: "the evolution of a central idea through continually changing circumstances." As you've already learned from earlier chapters in this book, during the early life of my company, I made many changes in details, tactics, and execution of my core idea as spelled out in my original business plan:

- ¢ I hired and fired until I had the right people in each job.
- ¢ I continually revised our target numbers upward.

- ¢ I changed my management approach from "business operator" to "CEO" by instituting systems and procedures, and by learning how to be hands-on without micromanaging.
- ¢ I added new services.
- ¢ I revamped departments, including departmental goals, methods, and accountability controls.

And we're not finished yet. My intention is for my company to remain a perpetual work in progress–a living, growing, organism. But despite our ongoing tactical and strategic changes, the core idea of the company has not changed. The ideas that I spelled out in the original Mission Statement, Key Principles, and Vision still apply: we remain committed to maintaining, growing, and creating financial wealth for our investors by treating the investors' money as if it were our own. And, I'm still determined to make our firm the biggest private money lending institution in America!

To Be a Maverick Millionaire, Learn to Love Change

Love of change is one of those crucial internal assets that make a person a Maverick Millionaire...and it's indispensable to becoming "maverick rich." Change is not only a useful corrective for your company; it's the emotional antidote to stagnation and boredom for you personally. The same applies to your employees. If you want to keep them, you need to keep them interested–and that means, change things!

Wealthy, successful people adapt easily to change. They don't resist it. Successful people recognize that change is not only necessary; it's healthy and even fun. They learn to view change as desirable because it means new experiences–new discoveries–and new achievements.

Companies, in one respect, are like sharks: either they keep moving forward, or they sink. Sure, I want my company to run like a Swiss watch. But that doesn't mean I want it frozen in place. What works beautifully this year will not be adequate to meet next year's needs. Maybe not even next week's!

As Winston Churchill liked to say: "To improve is to change. To be perfect is to change often."

Learn to love change.

Chapter 22:

To Be Decisive, You Must "Decide to Decide"

"Will somebody *please* make a decision?" That woeful cry is heard at every badly-run company in America. In a poorly managed shop, decisions either don't get made...or they don't get made in time to do any good...or they are made, but not communicated effectively to the staff...or they are always made "provisionally," which means they are subject to endless revisions, second-guessing and reversals. In other words, no real decision has been made at all.

In theory, making a decision is a simple matter of defining alternatives, evaluating their pros and cons, and selecting among them. Simple, perhaps, but not always easy.

An old story comes to mind...

A farmer takes on a hired hand to help with chores. On the first morning he tells the hand: "Hitch up the mule and go plough the back 40."

The job should take two days but shortly after lunchtime, the hand returns and says, "Okay, I'm finished."

The farmer is astonished to find all 40 acres perfectly ploughed and furrowed. He says: "Take this axe and go clear the trees from the bottomland I just bought."

By mid-afternoon hired hand comes back and again says, "Okay, I'm finished." The stunned farmer sees that every tree is cleared and all the wood is neatly stacked. The farmer thinks: This guy is a prodigy!

I'd better give him an easy job now, so I don't accidentally kill him from overwork.

The farmer says: "See that bin of potatoes? I want you to sit down and sort them. Good ones in this pile, bad ones in this pile, doubtful ones in this pile." The hand says okay, plops down on the stool, and begins sorting. The farmer leaves him for an hour.

When the farmer returns to check on progress, he finds the hired hand lying on the ground, passed out.

The farmer throws a bucket of water on the man to wake him up and demands: "What the hell is wrong with you? I leave you with an easy job, and I find you lying down?"

The hired hand groans: "Mister, I don't mind hard work. It's them DECISIONS that's killin' me!"

Decisions are indeed killers–*if* you don't know why, when, and how to make them. But making decisions, wisely and in a timely and effective fashion, is the main responsibility of a CEO. Lead, follow, or get out of the way!

NOT making decisions–the old dodges of dither, delay, and deny–are company-killers. When the staff doesn't know what direction they're supposed to go, they become demoralized. When there is no decision to implement, the company stagnates. When the boss hesitates to commit, he hands the competition a gilt-edged invitation to be first to market with a certain innovation (and that's half the battle).

Anyone whose management motto is "If it ain't broke, don't fix it" is begging to be blindsided. New conditions arise continually in this fast-changing economy, changes that obsolete existing strategies and policies. By the time "Mr. Don't Fix It" is willing to (grudgingly) concede that something is broken, the entire company may be damaged beyond repair.

This means the first step toward making a decision is "deciding to decide." You must elevate decisiveness to a prime value. You must vow that you will be a decisive leader who favors clarity over confusion, industry leadership over endlessly playing catch-up, and action over inaction.

From there, it's a three-step process: recognize when you have reached a fork in the road where a decision is necessary; gather information about consequences and alternatives; and finally select and commit.

Step 1. Recognition: When Do Decisions Become Necessary?

Realizing when a decision is called for can be difficult, but it's 10 times harder if the leader has a built-in bias against change. That tends to make him or her resistant to the very idea that a decision is necessary, even if the staff is begging for a decision or the need for change is staring everyone right in the face. Once again, the preliminary attitude of "deciding to decide" is invaluable.

What are the signs that a decision is necessary? Here are just a few.

For Individuals:

1) You feel inspired or excited about tackling some new challenge or achieving a new goal.
2) Someone close to you, whose judgment you trust, advises you to consider a major change in your life.
3) You keep running into the same problems over and over.
4) You have recently experienced a personal crisis–in health, work, finances, or relationships.
5) Everything in your life is working fine now, but you can look ahead to see serious changes in basic conditions are coming. Again, this can relate to work, health, finances, or relationships.
6) You come into good fortune–expected or unexpected–in some area of your life. A promotion, a new love, a new baby, a big tax refund or inheritance, an opportunity to move to an exciting new place or new career.
7) You feel that an important talent of yours is untapped, or an important area of your life is under-developed.
8) You're just not happy with some aspect of your current life situation.

For businesses, it's time to make a decision when:

1) Your partners or staff make a suggestion and ask for a decision.
2) The competition makes a move, or is probably preparing to make a move, that demands your response.
3) A major customer makes a request...or a complaint...

and you have to admit it makes a certain amount of sense.

4) A major factor in the market changes, for good or ill: customers; regulatory environment; technology; new competition; strength of demand; availability of supplies and raw materials; status of allies, vendors, or partners; the health of the economy; etc.

5) The company runs into a positive but unexpected change, such as when one sector of your business takes off when it's not "supposed" to…even when it's not the glamour sector, the flagship sector, or the traditional sector.

6) The company runs into an unexpected failure, even if it's the boss's pet project and lots of resources and prestige have been sunk into it.

7) You're not satisfied with the status quo. (In my opinion, you never should be satisfied with the status quo!)

8) You see an opportunity to grow or improve the company: a new product, new service, new market, new employee or position, an acquisition, merger, or sale…the list is endless.

9) A particular problem recurs repeatedly, and neither existing systems and procedures nor ad-hoc managerial intervention seems to solve it.

10) You have a nagging feeling that something, somewhere, is off-kilter. Further investigation reveals a mismatch between means and ends somewhere, or between performance and result, or a situation where existing operations are working reasonably well, but many people feel, "There ought to be a better way."

Each of these situations represents an opportunity in disguise. Opportunities call for *decisions* about whether and how to embrace them.

When I look at my own management style, I am most proud of being willing to face facts, and being willing to address issues as they come—IMMEDIATELY—with strong action. It takes a leader to do that. No company is flawless; every company in the world runs into surprises, changes, disappointments, scares, challenges, and both good and bad fortune—both internally and externally.

The most successful people see these situations as opportunities, not problems, and act upon them. The most successful companies have leaders who hit these situations head-on. If something doesn't look right, I dig into it, find out what's happening and why, and work with my team to deal with the situation. This is empowering and the more you do it, the more you build self-confidence and confidence, in your own mind and in the minds of the people around you. If you don't take this approach, you are leaving your destiny up to the stars.

If the situation is an opening for my people to exercise their strengths, I follow up promptly, enthusiastically, and aggressively. Every day, every hour, every minute that goes by that an opening is pursued nimbly, can represent stealing a march on the competition. If nothing else, a fast start can buy you (or your company) more time to reflect and maneuver later on, down the road. It's a false statement to say you "can't buy time." Of course you can...by getting the greatest possible head start on every situation.

On the other hand, if the situation to be dealt with is a problem (internal or external), I don't like it any more than anybody else–but I do like getting it off my agenda. Every day, every hour, every minute that goes by that a problem is not dealt with, is a lost opportunity.

Step 2. Education: Lay Out Options, Analyze, Evaluate

What Are My Options?

When you suspect that a major move may be necessary, and realize that a major decision may be called for, DO NOT assume that you automatically see all the options. This early period of relative uncertainty is preeminently the time for staff consultation, either one-on-one or in wider meetings. If it's a truly big decision with potentially serious consequences, it may also be an excellent time to consult your mentors, peers, and outside experts.

Ask for options. It's no sin if you don't think up all the possible options yourself. An inspired leader may see an option that nobody else does, and when that happens, it's great. It can lead to a creative and organizational breakthrough that revolutionizes a company, an industry, or the world. But it's also a sign of strong leadership to be able and willing to ask your key people for options. Most of the time, then, the list of options should be compiled through a process of discussion, brainstorming, and consultation.

For example, I recently conferred with one of my top staff regarding a problem. Dealing with that individual instance was fairly routine, but I realized the situation could call for a new policy to prevent or reduce the likelihood of repeating this problem in the future.

Instead of saying to my employee: "We're going to pass along the costs of this problem," I asked: "What can we do about this? What are our other options? What do you think about it? How would it affect our rapport with our market if we pass along the cost to someone else in the market chain?"

Her response was useful and constructive. She agreed with some of my suggestions, and had alternative approaches for others. We came to a compromise that we both felt comfortable with and instituted a new policy.

When to Heed Expert Counsel—And When to Ignore It

Earlier in this book I've given many examples of cases where I turned to my mentors for advice and counsel, to help me make a decision. I also confer with accountants, lawyers, and PR/marketing experts–if I'm dealing with situations where their specialty applies. However, I bear in mind that advice is just that: advice.

Lawyers, accountants, and marketers come with their own built-in biases that may not actually be best for the company. At times, it's the smart move to borrow $85 million, even if it makes your accountants very, very nervous—as Martha Stewart discovered. Likewise, marketing experts may not know squat about John Q. Public's tastes and desires, despite reams of customer survey data and focus group feedback. (If you don't believe me, just ask the people who persuaded the Coca-Cola Company to drop what is now known as Classic Coke in favor of the short-lived, disastrous experiment known as New Coke.)

The only person with the broad perspective required to make the right decision for you, is YOU. A good leader can appreciate all the complexity in a complex situation, and yet reduce them to a few essentials. Some people view that as a gift, but I believe it's a skill that can be cultivated and strengthened. You have to work at it. You have to realize that often, how you "frame" the issue will determine how you finally decide to handle the issue.

In the middle of a recession, should Boeing risk billions in R&D, production, and marketing costs to launch a new model that handles hundreds of passengers and can fly halfway around the globe? If the decision is framed in the context of, "Above all, minimize risk" or "Let's wait until we see proven demand for similar products," then the answer is no. If the decision is framed in the context of, "Air travel is growing but the number of airports is not keeping up; and we want to beat the competition with the most cost-effective possible commercial jetliner," then the answer is the Boeing 777, which is rewriting aviation history every day.

If I get advice that I feel is contrary to what I view as best for my company, I don't just blow it off. I get a second, third, or fourth opinion. If you're not comfortable with the advisor or advice you're getting, check around. If you hear the same thing three, four, five times, then you may have to accept that perhaps this repeated message is correct. "Well, I've gone to four experts in the legal field and they're all telling me the same thing...so even though I didn't want to hear this, maybe now it's time to listen

Put It On Paper!

One of the oldest decision-evaluation procedures in the book is still one of the most effective: draw up a list of options, on paper. Then make a list of the pros and cons of each option, also on paper.

Sometimes the sheer length of the pros or the cons will surprise you. What had previously seemed a complex, agonizing decision suddenly becomes a no-brainer.

At other times, you may realize that what you originally believed to be a long list of pros is actually just one advantage, restated several different ways. Looking at things on paper can really shift the balance of your evaluation.

Should You Follow Your Head, Or Go With Your Gut?

A crucial part of the process of evaluating your options is to listen to the voice in your own head...or the feeling in your own gut, as the case may be. Billionaire investment guru George Soros (The Quantum Fund) and Sony co-founder Akito Morita both said they have the same decision-making style: they "swallow the deal," go home and sleep on it. The next morning when they wake up, they literally let their gut decide. If their stomach feels good, they go with the deal. If they have a queasy feeling, they turn it down.

Amazing. Here are some of the world's most powerful CEOs, running top business empires, talking about making some of their biggest, most important decisions based on gut instinct!

I think making gut decisions is a great thing to do, when you have the experience to do it. Business tycoons on the level of Soros and Morita who make these gut decisions, have probably done 20 other deals just like this one before. They have seen what's gone right, what's gone wrong, and the crucial factors that spell the difference between success and failure.

They let all these facts and accumulated experiences sink down inside them and percolate. The next morning when they wake up and have a "gut feeling," it's not necessarily just an emotion or a pure, out-of-the-blue intuition. It's a deep conviction that comes from their subconscious mind digesting all this other information, comparing it to past and present experiences. It's waiting for an answer out of a calculator: you input the data as usual, but instead of spitting out the result instantly, the answer arrives the next morning–in your gut!

The opposite approach, taking the percentage play and going with cool calculations and logic, is advocated by billionaire Warren Buffett. He says his "road to Damascus" experience as an investor came at age 19 when he read a book *(The Intelligent Investor)* that helped him realize that investment decisions could be made with sheer intellect as the final arbiter. The experience was so powerful that Buffett still recalls it sharply, 50 years later. "I don't want to sound like a religious fanatic or anything, but it really did get me," he says. "Prior to that, I had been investing with my glands instead of my head."

Deciding "how" to decide—with the head, the heart, the gut...by yourself, or letting "experts" make the call for you—is a crucial part of deciding. You shouldn't let your gut decide an important call, unless and until you have decades of experience!

Step 3. Commit:
Select; Announce; Assign; Act

The actual act of making a decision is where the rubber meets the road. You select what you believe is the best option, inform the appropriate staff, and instruct them as to what they must do–and what resources and authority you are giving them–to carry out their part in the decision.

It's not enough to decide on the end; you have to figure out the means, as well. "You haven't made a decision until you've found a way to implement it," says management expert Peter Drucker.

So parents should not just announce, "We're going to plant a new garden in the front yard, everybody"–and then drive off to a picnic in the park. Likewise, business leaders should not announce, "We're going to launch a manufacturing division"–and then take off for a six-month vacation in Hawaii, with no plans in place to make it happen. In both cases, that is not a decision to innovate; it's a decision to abdicate!

If you're going to launch anything new, from a family garden to a corporate manufacturing division, then you need to sit down with your team and map out a *strategy.* That, happily, puts us back on the familiar ground of "Where are we now? Where do we want to go? How will we get there? How will we monitor our progress? How will we adjust our tactics in midstream?"

Appoint someone to be in charge of carrying out the decision, or start taking concrete steps to carry it out yourself, or both. And then, get busy! As any reader of this book can tell by now, I am a big believer in action. Take an educated risk, see what happens, chalk up any failures to the ongoing process of education, and refine your approach the next time.

President Franklin D. Roosevelt, hailed today by many historians as "the savior of capitalism," expressed this entrepreneurial spirit as well or better than anyone before or since. FDR's strategy for defeating the Great Depression was nothing if not decisive.

Roosevelt once declared: "This country needs, and unless I mistake its temper, the country demands bold, persistent experimentation. It is common sense to take a method and try it. If it fails, admit it frankly and try another. But above all, try *something.*"

Spoken like a true leader!

As a child, I was never eager to go on roller-coaster rides. I was scared of being out of control. And so, although I loved flying, I was terrified of turbulence.

My mentor "George" introduced me to aerobatics: the art and science of putting your airplane through spectacular feats such as rolls and loops and flying upside down. I had always been attracted to the "idea" of aerobatics — but didn't know if I'd find the real thing a thrill, or if I would just throw up.

"George" was a big kidder. That first time, he didn't reveal in advance what he had in mind. I thought we were just going for a regular flight in his RV-6. So we're climbing off the runway at about 500 feet, doing 160 miles per hour, and without warning he executes a 90-degree turn. Slam! In two seconds we're pulling three-and-a-half G's (several times normal earth gravity).

"How does that feel?" George asked, laughing. Well, it felt like my whole head was spinning, but I was giggling like a little kid. George put the plane through its paces. When we landed, I knew I had to learn to fly aerobatics someday.

Later, another pilot showed me how to pull the airplane straight up, how to do a loop, hammerheads, and more. He introduced me to negative G's and snap rolls. He showed me an unlimited maneuver called the rolling turn, where the airplane is physically rolling right but you're actually turning left in a 360° circle. When I could afford it, I purchased an Extra 300L, the Ferrari of sports planes, and took lessons from Greg Poe, the "Top Gun" of aerobatic flight. Before long I became Greg's protégé and we started flying air shows together.

Aerobatic flying is where civilian pilots separate those with the "Right Stuff" from the also-rans. In business, the equivalent of this crucial dividing point comes when you decide to "go for it" and perform many forms of high-flying creativity.

To the uninitiated, it looks like a crazy stunt. To the pros, it's the essence of the whole exercise…and the reason why they got into the game in the first place.

Chapter 23:

YOU Create Opportunities

Opportunity, they say, is where you find it. Opportunity, I say, is where you *make it.* You certainly won't find it by sitting around waiting, hoping, and wishing for it–and it won't find you, either. But the moment you decide to take responsibility for making things happen, you'll see opportunities all around you.

As a wise man once explained: *"When you change the way you look at things, the things you look at change."* To be absolutely clear, this doesn't mean you look at different objects and situations. It means that you see the same objects and situations that you saw before, only now you see them in a whole new way.

That, in a nutshell, is the whole secret of finding–or more accurately, making–opportunity.

A $25 Start-Up Becomes a $20,000,000 Empire

Frank Seninsky was a young engineering student at Stevens Institute of Technology when he bought an old used pinball game for $25 and installed it in his fraternity house. Set on 10¢ per play, the unit earned $150 over its first weekend. On Monday, Frank's frat brothers asked him to bring in a second pinball game.

Calculating that his return on investment would be realized in three days or less, Frank quickly provided games to all the fraternities on the Stevens campus–as well as Rutgers University and the New Jersey Institute of Technology.

Within two years, he was operating games in more than 50 fraternities and sororities. Since his company had started in a fraternity, he named it with Greek letters: Alpha-Omega Amusements.

That was 1970. Today, the still-youthful Frank Seninsky is running the

Alpha-Omega Group, a $20 million empire of several interlocking companies. These companies provide fun center design consultation, hi-tech equipment, marketing support, and technical services to the biggest theme parks and casinos in America, and to some of the glitziest resorts in the Caribbean and the oil-rich Middle East.

"Sometimes you have to create opportunity out of what appears to be thin air," says Seninsky. "The beauty of this approach is that the number of opportunities available to you is limited only by your own vision and imagination. That's why I maintain there is plenty of opportunity and growth potential at all levels of the American economy today."

Those who know Frank say his big problem is keeping up with all the new ideas and opportunities he creates–and deciding which ones to take a pass on.

The trick, says Frank, is setting your mental wavelength to a receptive channel. That means seeing things with fresh eyes and an open mind. "It's certain that we will never notice the wealth of opportunities that surround us, if we spend seven days a week plodding along the same well-worn path we have been traveling for years," he says. "As we look around for opportunities and growth potential in today's market, we can find them almost everywhere. The market is teeming with wonderful possibilities."

Frank Seninsky's example shows why opportunities are extraordinary things to those people who do not understand them, but they are normal occurrences in the lives of those who do understand them. Opportunities are nothing more than situations in your life that you choose to take advantage of. Not magical, extraordinary coincidences...I am talking about ordinary, run-of-the-mill experiences!

Definition of a Business Opportunity

It's important to realize just what an opportunity really is. The oldest business advice in the world instructs us to "find a hole (a need) and fill it." Peter Drucker, the late, great management consultant, said the purpose of business is "to CREATE a customer."

Combining these two insights, Frank Seninsky *found a need* for entertainment at his college fraternity, fulfilled it, then went out and *created more customers* at colleges across the region—and then at theme parks and casinos around the world.

I *found a need* for specialized financial services when some private lenders in Las Vegas asked me to handle their accounts. After founding Diamond Bay Investments, I quickly went on to create *my own, much-expanded customer base* through advertising, marketing, and word of mouth–all classic forms of client recruitment.

Rememver, wealth is a choice. Choosing to become wealthy is the precondition for seeing opportunity all around you. If you truly make that choice and commit yourself to it, it's like putting on a special pair of glasses that reveal things you never saw before. After all, if your hobby is riding horses, you'll think about horseback riding all day. When a friend suggests a trip to the country, you will instantly think: "Maybe I'll get a chance to go trail riding."

If your passion is aviation, you'll think about airplanes and helicopters all day. When you're driving down the highway and you see a police chopper overhead, you won't wonder: "Is that 'eye in the sky' doing a radar check on my speed?" Instead you'll think, "Hmm, wonder how many hours that pilot has?"

Likewise, if you're zealous about becoming wealthy, your mind will naturally run in that direction at the least provocation. It's not greedy or obsessive; it's just the way our minds automatically work. So, tune your mind to the "wealth channel," put on your "opportunity glasses," and get ready to discover a whole series of Golden Opportunities every time you walk, drive, gallop–or fly–across town.

In a World of Goliaths, There's Still Plenty of Room for Davids

Some people believe that today's world has become so complex that only large, well-funded organizations can succeed. These people assume that no small, shoestring-financed independent can become a thriving start-up. They claim: "Sure, you could start an empire on a $25 investment way back in the Dark Ages of the 1970s, but it can't be done today. Nowadays, you must have deep pockets, a big staff, and heavy-duty marketing clout from Day One."

This is total and complete nonsense.

Yes, some companies begin with tremendous resources at their disposal. But most new U.S. companies still begin in a garage, den, or small office, with little or no capital. Nearly every entrepreneur I know in the "young CEOs" networking association started that same way: one person, small company. Eventually they hired one more person to help them out. Then another, then a couple more, until they ended up growing their businesses into something impressive. Again, what's needed is the ability to see an opportunity…a "hole" that you can fill.

Here are three randomly chosen examples of people who recently started a company with little or no capital. Within three years, their local branches of the U.S. Small Business Administration honored each of them as "Entrepreneurs of the Year":

¢ After Gary Jessen graduated from the University of Washington, he decided to turn his senior class project into a business. Plumb Serve offered same-day, 24-7 plumbing service to customers in three counties around Greater Seattle. Next to a stunningly obvious idea, his greatest asset may have been an unforgettable slogan: *"We'll Be Out Today Or You Don't Pay!"* Starting from scratch, it took Gary three years to grow his revenues 700%. Today he runs a $2 million business employing 15 people.

¢ When Rebecca Flores became a mother at age 21, she wanted to work at home and figured other young professionals—including stay-at-home parents, the disabled, and students—might have the same need. That year she founded Mobile Office Assistants out of Buena Park, CA. Turns out, Rebecca tapped into a gold mine: an army of highly-qualified temps who could do almost any kind of office support work, online. MOA's "virtual assistants" now provide marketing, legal support, mass mailings, mobile notary public services, Spanish translations, transcription, and word processing. MOA has doubled its growth each year for the first four years and, at last report, was poised for another year of stellar expansion.

¢ Aaron Simmons was walking down a street in Miami, admiring the palm trees, when "This idea just popped in my head," he says, "...to create a planter to place around trees. It's a simple concept. It gives the illusion that the trees growing out of the ground are actually growing out of the pot." He patented his concept and launched a website to market it. Now that he's generated one successful idea, this onetime art major suddenly sees a forest-full of possibilities. Says Aaron: "I'll never be able to finish everything in my head and I'm only 29."

Aaron's horticultural venture suggests another important lesson in seeing (and seizing) opportunity. You grow a business the same way you grow a garden. You don't plant a seed, then come outside the next day and start eating strawberries! You plant, you water a little, you shuffle the soil a bit. You create better conditions for growth. You water it some more. And then one day you have a ripe piece of fruit.

That is how business works: it must be given a chance to grow over time. Most companies don't start big and grow bigger. They grow from small to large. What makes this growth happen is the person leading the company, making the right decisions, taking the right actions.

That means the chief asset is YOU! Remember, you are not starting with nothing; you are starting with talent, drive, intelligence, passion, hopefully a great idea, and unlimited potential. Successful entrepreneurs understand this from Day One, and they begin their businesses with the happy realization that *"The destiny of this company depends on me. Nobody else can make it happen–and by gosh, I am absolutely DETERMINED to MAKE it happen!"*

Oh, I suppose a person could always wait for the heavens to open wide, a heavenly light to shine down upon his or her shoulders, the seas to part, and to be blessed with wealth and wisdom–effortlessly.

But it would be an awfully long wait.

So instead of depending on the fates to hand you the opportunity of a lifetime, why not go out and envision it...invent it...create it? This responsibility is empowering, not a burden. The successful entrepreneurs are those who take action on a daily basis to grow their company and move it forward.

They *create* opportunity.

Chapter 24:

Don't Negotiate!

(But if You Must, Here's How)

I have a confession to make: I hate negotiation. The very word "negotiation" makes me grit my teeth. Maybe it's the unique slant that I put on the word. To me, negotiation is a code word for "haggling over prices"–an activity that I find highly unappetizing. In fact, I despise the whole picture of union and management, yelling at each other across opposite sides of a long rectangular table, banging their fists and threatening walk-outs or firings. In cases like these, negotiation means playing a high-stakes game of chicken that, all too often, nobody really wins.

On the other hand, when you say "negotiation" if you're talking about potential partners sitting around a (round) table, creatively brainstorming...generating exciting ideas about what they can mutually contribute to a joint project...or how they can make a deal productive and rewarding for both parties...I'm your man.

If by "negotiation" you mean a loving husband and wife coming up with a creative plan to balance their work and home responsibilities, I'm all for it. If "negotiation" means members of a scouting troop, a community services organization, or an exercise class finding ways to give and take, working together to improve their lives, I support that enthusiastically.

Sometimes, the first type of negotiation (haggling over prices) is inevitable, but for the most part my advice is: don't negotiate. In a personal relationship or a community situation, simply give whatever you can give, or believe it is right to give. Lead by example and the other party will either be inspired to follow your model, or–if not–then you can live with simply doing what you think is right.

In a business situation, find out what the market rate is for goods or services (it's not exactly difficult), and pay it without complaining. If your purpose is to retain the services of a uniquely valuable employee or team, or to ensure the supply of a high-quality, indispensable product, pay above market rate. I don't understand how anyone could have a problem with this approach. For goodness' sake, you're not paying ransom–you're making a solid investment in your company. You ensure getting the commodity (goods, labor). Just as important, you ensure good will. How can you beat that?

Remember, the rule of thumb in life, and in business, is that a good deal is one where everybody wins…and the win-win scenario is moral because it serves the greater good. Few acts are as destructive as entering a negotiation with the attitude, "I don't win, unless YOU lose." This attitude is not only destructive to the other party; ultimately it is destructive to your side, too. You can easily win the battle but lose the war by putting the "opposition" over a barrel, forcing them to make painful concessions, and then gloating about it.

Some victory! All you have achieved is to make an enemy who will be looking for payback at the earliest possible moment. In many cases, he'll find a way to inflict it–either directly or indirectly. Do you believe that word of mouth creates the best advertising? If so, then consider what kind of advertising you create with a "take no prisoners" style of negotiation.

Jordan Wirsz? Oh, man, he's a tough negotiator. He'll take you for every last dime you've got. Then he'll hang you upside down and shake you to see if any pennies fall out of your pockets.

Potential partners and customers will stay away in droves!

If Adversarial, Negotiations Are Unavoidable

When "highly competitive" or even hostile negotiations are unavoidable, the most constructive way to win is a four-step process:

(1) Know your own bottom line or least-acceptable resolution. Be prepared to insist on it. Be prepared to explain it. At length. Convincingly. And politely!

(2) Gather *excellent* intelligence on the situation (the law, the market, the politics, whatever) and on the other party's needs, desires, and probable bottom line.

(3) Keep your cool. Never, ever get emotional and don't let your ego become invested in the outcome, good or bad. Remember that win or lose, you want to stay friends with the other side when it's all over, if possible.

(4) Never compromise on your pre-determined limitations.

I don't have much experience with high-stakes, high-pressure, price-haggling type negotiations–both because costs in my business are fairly standardized, and due to my strong personal dislike for "us-versus-them" type bargaining.

However, some of my friends and peers have racked up a great deal of experience in adversarial negotiations. From their war stories, I gather that the critical step in the above process is often phase two (intelligence).

The most impressive example I know of intelligence-gathering in business negotiations is a story about a CEO of my acquaintance. This man–let's call him Roger–once handled a negotiation and won total, complete, and absolute victory. That is, he not only got the other side to agree to its ultimate, bottom-line, lowest acceptable price–he also remained on friendly terms with the other party, after signing a deal that was highly favorable to his side.

If anything, Roger strengthened this rapport with the other party precisely because of his tough-but-fair negotiating stance. His partners in the deal were blown away by Roger's uncanny business acumen. During the negotiation process, he seemed instinctively to understand their "cards" and to play his own hand with unerring skill.

Every time the other party tried to get Roger to budge off their bottom-line price (or any other minimal condition), he politely but firmly refused. He would not give an inch, period. And, he patiently waited them out, through days and days of attempts by their side, until the other party finally gave up and agreed to his terms. They made money, too, but not as much as they'd hoped for.

How did Roger do it?

The other party was a foreign company and the negotiations took place at their headquarters, in their host nation. The date for the big negotiation was set months in advance. Before flying there, Roger took a crash course in that country's language. By the time negotiations began, he wasn't as fluent as a diplomat, but he was conversant enough to understand much of what he heard.

Naturally, Roger didn't tell his hosts (the other party in the negotiation) that he had learned their language. They assumed he was just another ignorant American. As a result, during the negotiation sessions–and in Roger's presence–the members of the host company lapsed into their own language and spoke with complete freedom, just as if they were alone. As the members of the other party debated tactics, revised their positions, and agreed among themselves what their bottom-line position was on each agenda item, Roger heard every word. And kept a poker face.

No wonder he went home with all the marbles.

Don't Get Emotional!

I understand the consequences of this directive extremely well, because I am guilty of violating it at least once. At age 19, I walked into a car dealership to buy a Mitsubishi Diamante. They were advertising a great deal: no money down, zero interest for 12 months. I wanted that deal. I entered with a businesslike mindset that I knew my bottom line and was determined that I would stick to my guns. I test drove the car and fell in love with it. I told myself, there is no other car that has these features for this price. When I returned to the dealership, they said: sorry, Jordan, but you have limited credit.

I sputtered: "What do you mean? I have great credit. In fact, at 19 years old I have credit cards with $25,000 credit limits!"

They said, well, you don't have more than three years on the credit bureaus, so you get an interest rate of 12.99% and nine months with no payments on the principal, but you *must pay interest* during that nine-month period. I got hot about it, but they didn't budge. They knew I was a kid, and they knew I wanted that car. That means they knew I wasn't going to walk out of there. In the end, I bought the car for more than retail price. I allowed myself to get taken.

I walked away kicking myself and saying: damn it, if I hadn't fallen in love with that car…if I hadn't gotten so emotional, feeling that I had to have that car, that it was the only car that would make me happy…I would have been fine. In fact, if I had walked way, they probably would have called me a day later and said: we reconsidered and we're going to bend some rules; we'll give you the deal you want.

When your ego is on the line, your emotions become involved. When you get upset, it changes your state of mind. Getting mad, getting frustrated, and visibly showing it makes you weaker, not stronger, in any negotiation. Getting emotional puts you at a disadvantage.

This lesson applies to every aspect of life. A "deal" or subject for negotiation can be asking your spouse to take the kids for a night, buying a home, deciding who sings the solo this week in the church choir, or which parents drive the kids to Little League this week. A deal may also involve buying a house, acquiring a company, or asking the boss for a raise. All are deals; all require a certain amount of negotiation.

The way to take the emotion out of the deal, is to take *yourself* and your ego out of the picture. Step back and look at it dispassionately, as if your best friend were buying the car or negotiating the deal. What would you advise him or her? That's what you should do, on your own behalf. Few people have the skill or objectivity to look at a deal that way. But you must be able to say: the outcome of this negotiation does not reflect on me personally. If it succeeds and we make a deal, it's because this was "in the flow" and it was right for both of us. If it fails and we don't make the deal, I don't lose face–I just accept that our mutual karma wasn't hitting on all cylinders at this time, and I go on to the next opportunity.

Therefore, I am prepared to "lose" the negotiation, if by losing you mean–not getting the deal at all.

Paradoxically, being perfectly prepared to lose, puts you in the strongest position to win. This is why Herb Cohen, one of America's foremost business negotiators and the author of "You Can Negotiate Anything," always recommends: "Care–but not too much."

MAVERICK MOTIVATOR:

Self-employed = happier work. The self-employed are considerably more satisfied with their jobs than are other workers, according to a Pew Research Center poll of 2,003 Americans ages 18 and over. They're more satisfied with their salaries, the job security, chances for promotion, level of on-the-job stress, flexibility of hours and proximity of work and home.

Steve Appleton, Micron Technology: Negotiating From Strength

Sometimes, research and intelligence gathering are not the keys to successful negotiation. The key is knowing your own bottom line, and being willing to insist on getting it–especially when you hold some of the aces in the deck.

Steve Appleton of Micron Technology told me about one of his most high-wire negotiating dramas–one that captured the attention of the business world a decade ago, when this hi-tech leader was a $3 billion firm. "My own Board fired me for eight days in 1996," Steve recalls. "I was 36 years old, the third youngest CEO of a Fortune 500 company at the time." He took it in stride. Calmly, he began making plans to move to a state where he had family and to enjoy a biplane flying vacation in Australia.

But before any of that happened, Steve got a surprising phone call midway through the week that followed his firing. As he tells it:

"The executive team called to say: we want you to come talk to us. We think the Board made a mistake; we believe they want you to come back. I said no, I can't work in that environment. All of the politics don't work for me. They said, we've put our jobs on the line. We told the Board what we thought of them. In fact, 22 of the 25 execs at the two sister companies said they'll resign if you don't come back. So that means if you don't come back, we'll be fired."

Steve agreed to talk to them.

At this point, Steve realized he held a very strong hand. The Board would either ask Steve to return–and address his concerns to induce him to return–or risk losing 88% of their senior management. There was a very good chance, he realized, that the Board would make some very significant concessions in order to avoid this potential catastrophe.

What happened next was a classic. Steve went in to face the Board and, not surprisingly, he says, "You could cut the tension in the air with a knife." The board offered him his job back, but the board also insisted Steve improve certain aspects of his management.

Shrewdly, Steve agreed. "I said: Fine, I've never thought I couldn't improve. But," he added, "I have a couple of requests too."

Steve's biggest demands were, first, employment contracts for all of his senior management so they couldn't be fired at-will, as he had been; and–the big one–the Board had to put a muzzle on one of its own members. This was a person who had, in Steve's description, tried to run the company without authority from the Board. As Steve put it, "This director did not know the difference between governance and management."

The Board balked at both demands, but Steve held firm. "I said look, neither item is negotiable. I understand agreeing to this is difficult, but in order for me to return, we must do these two things."

The Board then met without Management.

The Board had several factors to consider. The company's productivity was in chaos, and had been since the day Steve was terminated. A stockholders meeting was coming up in a few days. The replacement CEO was already having a nervous breakdown from the environment and the pressures of the job. The Management team was threatening to exit.

During a follow-up meeting with the Board a few hours later, Steve reminded them of all that he had to offer (and implicitly, of all that they had to lose). He looked directly at the most powerful member of the Board, and said: "I'll take care of the shareholder meeting. The stock price won't collapse. The executives will stay. Everyone will go back to work. All you have to do is agree to these two things. I think that's pretty reasonable."

Steve continues: "He looked at me, put his head down and said quietly: Okay." At that point, the rest of the Board easily agreed, said Steve: "The employment contracts were drawn up and signed that night. The executives and I handled the shareholder meeting, a standing-room-only event with 1,500 people packed into the convention center here in Boise,

Idaho. It was wild."

After having been bad-mouthed in the press for eight straight days, Steve particularly enjoyed the headlines in the local newspaper:

APPLETON IS BACK!

Very soon after that, the member of the Board who had caused most of the friction resigned in an emotional, impulsive way…removing the biggest thorn from Steve's side.

Today, Steve's perspective on the entire episode is very philosophical. "I learned how to work with a Board," he says simply. "I'm a much better CEO for it today." He adds that while he loves Micron, he loves other things too. "I'm not an emotional guy" when it comes to business, he allows.

What a powerful object lesson. Even when the deal appears to be about you, it's almost never about you. If you can muster the maturity to remember that, then you will win either way–if you go home with a deal, or without one.

Chapter 25:

Graduate-Level Brainstorming

My earlier chapter on meetings discussed how some of the best internal company conferences have a brainstorming agenda, and how to conduct such meetings. But an afternoon of tossing wild ideas around the conference room is only the kindergarten level of brainstorming. Now it's time to tackle the grown-up version:

- $ The Master Class in brainstorming extends this activity from inside one company, to an activity that makes sparks jump between two (or more) companies.
- $ The graduate level seminar takes brainstorming from the mind of the single individual, to the creative depths of the infinite.

Let's start with the Master Class: brainstorming as an inter-corporate activity. I'll give two quick examples: one "anonymous" historical story and one up-to-the-minute anecdote with (corporate superstar) names attached.

Example One: *Keiretsu* Ahead of its Time

Some years ago, a certain U.S. sales executive was struck with a huge inspiration for how to make the biggest sale of his career. In fact, if he pulled it off, it would be the biggest sale of anyone he'd ever met.

His idea wasn't just an ordinary delivery of goods and services. It would mean convincing one of his major customers to completely rethink and restructure some of their basic operations. It would mean permanently integrating the salesman's company with the client's company in a revolutionary new way, somewhat in the spirit of Japan's *keiretsu* (a combination of allied businesses that all do business with each other, individually and collectively). But this was long before such intimately cooperative group enterprises were dreamed of in the U.S. economy.

The salesman didn't breathe a word about his idea to his supervisor, because he knew what the boss would say: "Are you crazy? Don't you dare even suggest such an insane idea to our customer! We'll lose their business."

So the salesman went about developing the specifics of his proposal quietly, on his own time, in the evenings and on weekends. He largely dropped his other hobbies, recreation, and outside activities. "The Deal" became his hobby, his recreation, his passion. He didn't see this as a sacrifice; every time he thought about "The Deal," he felt a sense of quiet but profound excitement and pleasure.

He was meticulous. He carefully thought through every angle, calculated every cost and benefit, and gradually worked up a comprehensive master proposal.

This process took two full years.

Finally, the salesman was ready. Without telling his own company, he made an appointment to meet with the leadership of his customer's company. He knew that he was putting his own job on the line–if his proposal were rejected, he would surely be fired.

His customers listened to his presentation and, to put it mildly, they were blown away.

Next came plenty of follow-up meetings. The salesman's company was brought into the dialog, and together both companies engaged in lots of creative give-and-take. They considered inventive, alternative concepts for integration and cooperation. Endless details had to be ironed out. But excitement remained high and, within a year, the broad outlines of "The Deal" were accepted. The salesman's (by now) three-year project became reality.

Not long after that, he became president of his company–a job he had clearly earned.

This is brainstorming at its finest. As you can tell, the Master Class in brainstorming focuses on a long-term creative vision that eventually magnetizes the other party into your orbit, where you forge a new level of alliance and integration. The message of Master Class brainstorming is: "Look what I can do for you–and better yet, look what we can accomplish together!"

Example Two: Syrupy Synergy (With Cuddly Plush)

A very recent example of this type of brainstorming occurred when the Beverly Hills Teddy Bear Co. pitched a licensing concept to the Coca-Cola

Company. This is a true David & Goliath partnership, even though BHTBC is another one of those low-budget start-ups that zoomed from zero to $20 million in annual revenues in just eight years. That's an impressive achievement, but it still pales beside Coke's $22 billion annual sales.

CEO David Socha was still in his 20s when he invested three years, simply to persuade Coca-Cola to take a meeting and give him a serious hearing. Eventually, he broke through. He got make his pitch for an alliance, and then he got to forge the plush/syrup synergy of his dreams. Socha's line for Coke included various sized plush versions of Coke's polar bear and penguin characters, and "started a whole new beanie baby craze among Coca-Cola collectors," reports Coke execs.

"That was one where we said, strategically, they're the biggest brand in the world," Socha recounts. "We want to do something with them. So every few weeks, every few months, just call up. It's truly just the follow-through and the tenacity to not take no [for an answer]."

Of course, Socha's creative vision may have had a little something to do with the success of this brainstorming venture. The Beverly Hills Teddy Bear Co. thrived by inventing a unique niche in an overcrowded market, including "celebrity" plush. How sweet it is!

So much for the Master Class on brainstorming. Are you ready for the Graduate seminar?

The Mystical Secret Behind IBM's Famous Slogan

At the Graduate Level, business brainstorming can have almost mystical overtones. However, such brainstorming can have a revolutionary impact on you, on your company, and even on humanity itself. The example in this case is "Big Blue"–none other than International Business Machines.

Today, the world has largely forgotten that IBM president Thomas J. Watson Sr. originally intended to convey an entire system of philosophy with his famous one-word slogan, THINK. Under Watson's direction, the world's foremost data processing and (later) computer company displayed this slogan–without exception–in every IBM office and every IBM factory in 79 countries.

For decades, THINK was also emblazoned on every notepad that IBM executives and sales people used to scribble orders or ideas. THINK was the name of IBM's company magazine, published monthly to the tune of 100,000 copies and distributed to IBM personnel and "civilians" worldwide. THINK was engraved on the steps leading up to the classroom of the official IBM School in Endicott, New York.

People outside the company sometimes made fun of the slogan, but few ever understood what THINK symbolized to Watson. What is the forgotten secret behind this word? Fortunately, the historical record survives in one or two obscure places, and we can still learn transformational truths from this dynamic business leader.

At the height of his career, Watson engaged an award-winning artist/philosopher (and successful former businessman) named Walter Russell to go around the country, giving motivational talks to IBM's executives and sales force. From 1927 to 1939, Russell delivered a series of lectures titled "THINK: The First Principle of Business Success." The purpose of the talks was to explain true thinking as Watson and Russell conceived it.

The introductory lesson Russell taught was that *human* dynamics works on the same principle as the second law of *thermo*dynamics: "For every action there is an equal and opposite reaction." Or, in people terms –what goes around, comes around.

Russell said: Look, when you throw a ball against a wall, it doesn't just stay there. It bounces back to you. If you catch the rebound, you get a double value out of the work of throwing that ball.

How does this apply to business? Very simple–if you make one sale with your eye on the short-term profits from that one transaction, you are just throwing the ball across the yard. No bounce-back. Wasted energy.

However, Russell continued, executives who sincerely apply themselves to serving their customers, who put their customers first (that's the original throw at the wall) receive bigger benefits when their efforts "bounce back" to them back in terms of customer loyalty...repeat sales...positive word of mouth...and better mutual profits. That's the rebound, a sort of "dividend" on the original expenditure of energy.

This rather simple point was only the beginning, the set-up for what was to come.

The deep principle at work here, said Russell, is that "you and (your customer) are one." Now, some mystics believe the definition of love is recognizing others as a part of us, and vice versa. Russell appears to have been one of them. He surprised his hard-headed business audiences by telling them–with Tom Watson's enthusiastic approval–that if they wanted to make strong sales in the long run, they had better start by loving their customers as themselves...literally.

Sound familiar?

Yes, IBM's in-house motivational speaker was passing along Tom Watson's belief that observing the Golden Rule makes for sound business practice.

The old philosopher went on to say that Watson brainstormed about IBM, using precisely the same quasi-mystical inspirational process that artists use to create great paintings or symphonies. "The Watsonian Principle," explained Russell, "is the philosophy [that stresses]...the inward direction of his thinking"...in other words, a meditative process of going to the infinite "fountainhead" of all creative ideas.

As Russell described it, Watson had an almost religious purpose for IBM: not to put profits first, but to uplift the people who worked for the company and, consequently, to help uplift civilization itself! Russell proclaimed:

> *"IBM is Mr. Watson's instrument, upon which he interprets his purpose...Mr. Watson knew that he could create a super-organization of supermen only by increasing their thinking power and inspiring them with greater knowledge and comprehension. He also knew that very few people 'THINK' (they confuse conditioned reflexes and habit with original thinking)...Mr. Watson knew that people could be taught to think, even to the point of developing the latent genius which is within every man. That is why he posted that auto-suggestive word 'THINK' everywhere throughout his organization, and then instituted certain orderly procedures which compelled his men to think."*

Russell, a self-taught artist, was at one time the official portrait painter for President Teddy Roosevelt's family. A later president, Franklin D. Roosevelt, commissioned Russell to create two of the most important sculptures associated with his Administration (those are just a few of his amazing accomplishments). Russell believed that all human beings have untapped creative potential, which we can bring to fruition if only we know how.

"My responsibility," Russell told the IBM workforce, "is to awaken that something within you which comes from the inside, and which you have always had. I refer to your divine inheritance of those nitro-glycerin-like qualities of inspiration, imagination, vision and creative thinking power which measure each man's greatness to the extent in which he can be stirred into explosive action. I cannot give to you this power which lies behind creative action, but I can make you aware of it; and that is my sole purpose of being here."

Russell taught IBM employees that the creative process begins well before the actual introduction of any new idea into the workplace or the marketplace–much earlier than many people believe. Every successful new business idea, he said, requires a careful cultivation and gradual development–like the seed of an oak tree germinates in the ground for many months before it sprouts, or as an embryo silently and gradually develops inside its mother for many months before it is born.

Russell recommended that business people (or anyone else) who wish to tap their creativity to the fullest, should follow these key steps:

1) Decide to create a certain result–and commit to it completely.
2) Study and master the specific techniques needed to execute the plan, until they become as much a part of you as breathing. This means that, like a great musician, if you don't have to think about *how* you're playing your instrument; you can focus 100% on *what* you're playing: the melody that is your creative expression.
3) Allow the concept to germinate in your subconscious–for months or years, if necessary–until it is fully developed. "Too many salesmen go off half-cocked before they have worked out a good idea," Russell said. "They thereby waste what could have been a great concept."
4) Conserve energy by not dissipating it in a quest for endless stimulation and pointless distractions outside of your creative goal or your immediate work. (By the way, many creative and inspirational leaders from Beethoven to Gandhi have made this same point.)"This is a creative universe," Russell declared. "Creative ideas flow out from within. Only the form of the idea comes from without. Inspired creators look to the fountains which effervesce within them for their ideas. They then look outside of themselves for the materials with which to assemble those ideas into form."

He summarized: "Inspiration is more *necessary* in business than knowledge itself, for knowledge can be hired...but inspiration cannot."

Watson's son, who succeeded him as president of Big Blue, said his father once listed the top assets for a businessperson as "Vision, Unselfishness, and Love." No wonder IBM's official history describes Tom Watson Sr. as a leader with "evangelical fervor" who "preached a positive outlook" and a strong ethic of customer service! No wonder, too, that IBM quadrupled its revenues to about $9 million during Watson's first four years as company president.

Given the Watson-Russell philosophy, it's also not surprising that during the Great Depression years (while Russell was IBM's in-house motivational speaker), Watson managed to grow IBM while the rest of the economy tanked.

Finally, like all great ethical business leaders, Watson put his money where his mouth was. While many U.S. companies were cutting back, laying off, or closing down, IBM was among the first corporations to provide group life insurance, survivor benefits, and paid vacations way back in the 1930s. (That's straight out of IBM's own official history, too.)

Co-Creation Is the Most Fun You Can Have In Business

I certainly don't claim that every business needs a leader with a messianic streak. But I do say that if you want to reach the aerobatic level of business operation, this is where it's at: creativity. Some people think, "Well, I'm just not creative," but I believe those people simply haven't given themselves a chance. In the right circumstances, with the right encouragement, anyone and everyone can have an original idea.

And if you can have one original idea, you can have a lot more of them.

Without getting too otherworldly about it, I can report from personal experience that cooperative strategizing with your partners is not only good for the bottom line–it's terrific fun. At my company, we find many opportunities to engage in this kind of brainstorming, even within the (highly regulated) sphere of borrowing and lending. When you, your customers, your suppliers, and your allies put your minds together in an open-ended quest for the Win-Win Scenario, the result can be a beautifully workable solution that makes everybody happy.

Let the brainstorms begin!

Phase 4:

You can't see the wind. But it's there...a vital, living force...powerful enough to hurl you through those "footless halls of air," or to lay waste to an entire city. As a pilot you can fight this force, or you can cooperate with it. But you had darned well better believe in it!

Eventually, after hours and hours and hours of flying, you reach a point where you become one with the airplane. When that engine turns over, you start to feel the vibrations coming up through your legs, into your chest, and out through your arms. That's it! Once you're airborne, you feel the air during flight. You sense the very molecules of air flowing over the wing and the fuselage, and intuitively you know how your craft will react to the slightest touch of the controls.

I can't really explain that oneness. It's intuition...a sixth sense.

Before flying a demanding aerobatic routine, a crucial part of your preparation is mental. A pilot has memorized his performance. Before actually climbing into the plane and executing it, he takes some quiet time to sit alone and visualize every turn...every spin...every loop, climb, and roll. This is precisely the same mental ritual that world-class figure skaters and gymnasts perform before trying for an Olympic Gold Medal. See it in your mind...do it in your mind...perfectly.

When the Blue Angels sit down to perform this preflight ritual, the atmosphere resembles a séance: hushed, almost sacred. Nobody is talking. Everyone's eyes are closed. They are moving their hands, just as they would move the stick, and they are calling out what they will say over the radio. Slowly, they visualize their airplanes maneuvering in perfect harmony, in tune with invisible forces of wind and gravity...transcending ordinary physical limits.

The greatest pilots in the world–from Lindbergh and Saint-Exupery, to Richard Bach and Greg Poe–all agree: flying is a deeply spiritual experience. Well, so is business! At the highest levels, believing in the unseen is required for programming your subconscious; achieving near-mystical inspiration; and achieving the most powerful forms of belief in yourself.

Chapter 26:

Programming Your Mind for Success

"A rock pile ceases to be a rock pile the moment a single man contemplates it, bearing within him the image of a cathedral."

—Antoine De Saint-Exupery
pioneering aviator, author of *The Little Prince*

We've talked in earlier chapters about the importance of having a vision and of setting goals, transforming a dream in our minds from wish to intent. Writing down your goal is saying to yourself that it's real. The physical act of writing, we said, helps you marshal your psychic resources.

In this chapter we'll talk about other tools to discover those visions and marshal those resources. The most important of these tools is programming your mind, which is something we all do, whether we realize it or not.

Have you ever heard someone say, "So-and-so lies so much, they are actually starting to believe it themselves"? Well, it is true this can happen. If you tell your mind something, whether it's true or false, and if you reinforce it, your mind will subconsciously make it a reality for you. So when you tell yourself "I will always live in poverty because I am not good enough to be wealthy," your mind will make you take actions that make that a reality. However, if you constantly and consistently tell yourself "I am better than poverty, I deserve more, and I am making it better for myself," then your mind will make you make that a reality, too.

You see, as psychological beings we all work with the same spiritual potentials and the same spiritual laws. You, me, my neighbor, we are all the same in this respect. How we choose to view ourselves, and how we choose to actualize our potential, are what make us different.

If you remember earlier in this book, I said that I made a choice to be a pilot, and I made a choice to be a millionaire. Both are choices. The ability to make conscious, positive choices is our own God-given ability…and it's the first and greatest step in programming our minds for success. We can choose to be mediocre or we can choose to be awesomely successful. Success or failure, excellence or mediocrity, are not results of a fate that befalls us, even though it may appear that way right now. (If it does seem to you that your long-term life story has made you a victim of fate, then that is a measure of how much spiritual growing remains for you to do.)

We make our *choice* of life-destiny on a daily basis, by the things that we tell ourselves consciously and subconsciously. You must stay consistent, be true and honest with yourself, about what and who you choose to be. If you tell yourself subconsciously that you are not worthy of success, it won't do any good to tell yourself (consciously) that you are worthy of the Nobel Prize. *Becoming aware of our own negative subconscious programming is one of the greatest challenges we face.* Take my word for it; almost every person on this planet is walking around with some unconscious beliefs that are holding him or her back from achieving their full potential.

Here is where mentors are invaluable. The best of them can gently make us aware of our assumptions, and point out patterns in our own thinking that we may not even see ourselves.

However, merely becoming "aware" of such patterns and assumptions is not sufficient to get rid of them. We have to work as hard at conditioning our minds to be healthy, as we do to condition our bodies to be healthy—if not harder. Otherwise, we'll slip right back into those old patterns, even if their existence has been pointed out to us, and even if we have agreed—intellectually—that the assumptions are there and the assumptions are wrong.

My own "psychological fitness program" is just as rigorous and routine as my physical fitness program. At a minimum, I engage in daily sessions of putting positive images into my mind. I program myself for success 10 or 20 minutes at a time, using affirmations and visualization.

I take some quiet time each morning to simply sit outside, commune with nature and with my own thoughts. This is my time to "just be." I don't focus on any problem or project in particular; the whole idea is to be fully awake and alert, yet open, receptive, and mentally still. It is a wordless reverie.

Masaya Nakamura, founder and chairman of Namco Ltd. in Tokyo, has always practiced the same spiritual discipline. This creative business leader whose company invented Pac Man and a hundred other video games recommended that each of us set aside a few minutes of every day to go off by ourselves and listen to the silence. That is where inspiration comes from, he said.

Thomas Edison said the same thing. So did IBM's Thomas Watson, so did Henry Ford, and Autodesk CEO Carol Bartz, and Famous Amos's Wally Amos, and countless numbers of other successful people!

When You Believe It, Then You'll See It

Having a vision of what you want to achieve is a terrific first step toward realizing your dreams. The next step is: *live in the vision.* Keep the image of your desire constantly central in your mind, vividly aflame with passion.

Again, although this advice may sound airy-fairy, this is the most down-to-earth, pragmatic counsel you can possibly follow. The toughest soldiers in the U.S. armed forces–Navy SEALS–are taught this technique in an incredibly physical way. They stand in freezing cold surf up to their chests, holding a heavy rifle over their heads, for hour after hour. Meanwhile their instructors are walking up and down the beach, shouting:

"Don't just 'wish' that you were warm and dry, sometime in the future! SEE YOURSELF as being right there next to a crackling fire, all hot and toasty–RIGHT NOW! Don't tell yourself that your arms are getting tired. SEE YOURSELF bursting with strength! Visualize balloons tied to your rifle, pulling it over your head!"

One SEAL who went through this training explained: "Your drill captains constantly urge you to see yourself already on the mountaintop, enjoying all the benefits. And you know, when you're standing there in that 35-degree water with your rifle over your head, once you start to visualize that fireplace and imagine the warmth and power coursing through your veins, a funny thing starts to happen. The rifle doesn't seem so heavy anymore. The water doesn't feel quite so cold. You catch yourself spontaneously thinking: I can do this!"

Wally Amos, creator of the Famous Amos brand and founder of a chocolate chip cookie empire, is a huge believer in the power of belief and visualization. Amos told radio host Mike Litman of *The Mike Litman Show:* "Visualization, imagination, imagining–it's all the same thing. We underestimate and underrate the power of visualizing what it is that we want."

Amos pointed out that each of us constantly visualizes our next step before we perform it: getting dressed, driving to work, making a phone call... According to Amos, the identical process of "conceive, visualize, believe, realize" that works for us in the moment or within a single hour as we perform these routine actions, can serve us over the long haul–days, months, years as we perform far more complex, more ambitious actions.

You may not see all the steps between where you are now and your ultimate goal. But that's okay. Did Edison foresee all the steps between conceiving the electric light and perfecting the first working light bulb? Of course not!

The point is, Edison kept the vision of the electric bulb strongly and clearly in his mind from the first instant...through more than 1,000 trials and tests...until his dream became reality.

Negative Feedback Can Serve As Positive Motivation

A dream, vision, or goal, can serve as positive motivation, inspiring us to get moving and keep going. But we will run into obstacles, and some will be downright unfair and unkind. That is when a successful person turns negative feedback into positive motivation.

The first African American to become a fighter ace was Lee Archer. During World War II, Lee was one of the legendary Tuskegee Airmen: the all-black squadron of pilots who flew red-tailed P-51 Mustangs in combat over Germany. Their main mission was escorting bombers on raids deep into enemy territory, fending off clouds of enemy Messerschmitts (fighter planes) that tried to shoot down the American bombers. The proud record of the Tuskegee Airmen is that–*alone* among all U.S. Army Air Corps units–they never allowed the enemy to get at one single bomber. They never lost a single B-25 on a single mission.

So let me ask you: do you think those guys had something to prove, or what?

As a pilot myself, I can only imagine the fierce courage these pilots displayed, day after day, putting their lives on the line to defend their country. However, I don't have to imagine the guts and determination that it took to get that all-black P-51 squadron up and running in front-line combat operations. The Airmen themselves have told us all about it.

Lee Archer flew 169 combat missions, for which he won 18 Air Medals, the Distinguished Flying Cross, and more. He explains: "I made the decision that I wanted to fly in World War II"–despite the segregated armed forces of that era, despite the prejudice that African-Americans weren't smart enough to be officers, and despite the widespread racism that meant whites would do almost anything to avoid taking orders from blacks. All of these obstacles only made Archer and his fellow African-American soldiers more determined to achieve their dream.

"If they hadn't let me into flight school, they would have had trouble with me," he says–his voice still ringing with intensity today. "You can't tell me I can't do something. I'm a hardhead on that. I had an internal belief that I was good enough for the Air Corps"–and he brooked no opposition in acting upon that belief.

After the war, Archer says he carried the same belief and determination into civilian life. "The military experience I had, good and bad, made me what I am," he declares. What it made him was, initially, a manager at General Foods, and later, the CEO of an immensely successful lending firm called North Street Capital Corporation. NSCC financed more than 70 companies including Beatrice Foods, which became America's largest black-owned business at the time under the leadership of Archer's NSCC co-founder, Reg Lewis.

Archer turned negative feedback into positive motivation in other realms, too. As an honored veteran of several wars back, he was invited to fly an antique plane over Houston, Texas, with the Confederate Air Force in one of the nation's largest air shows. At first, Archer coldly refused. Why in hell, he asked the CAF leaders, would I want to support anything named after the Confederacy, which fought to defend slavery?

He called back and accepted the invitation. Archer still had something to prove, and he proved it. At that air show, the CAF leaders announced they were changing the name of their organization to the *Commemorative* Air Force. The CAF also held a huge banquet to honor Archer and the Tuskegee Airman, thanking them for their courage–both in the air, and on the ground.

As a Man Thinketh, So Is He

That goes for women, too. Autodesk CEO Carol Bartz says: "I have this core belief that you can do anything if you try. That's why we release new versions of our core AutoCad program annually–because when people say it can't be done, I say: We can (do it), we just don't know how. So we learn."

The power of our minds and beliefs can take us to astounding places. Studies have shown when someone believes they are cured of cancer...or even if they simply engage in passionate, daily sessions of visualizing themselves as perfectly well...in a surprisingly number of cases, the cancer begins to remit. Why does this happen? Because the patient's vision is so vivid, their vision is so powerful, that their body reacts to it. Their healing system kicks into gear and changes the person's very cells, in order to make the physical facts correspond to the person's mental and spiritual image.

If you think it, it becomes so. In business, in relationships, and in life, you create what you focus your energy on. So focus wisely and deliberately...and put the limitless power of your mind to work.

Chapter 27:

The View from 10,000 Feet

Perhaps you've noticed that a subtle theme runs through this book. That theme is *balance*. Balance is the principle that keeps human beings upright and walking, safely and gracefully. Balance plays a role in flying, when the power of gravity is perfectly *balanced* against the lift created by an airplane's wings.

Balance also keeps us moving safely and gracefully toward success in our everyday lives. Just a few of the balancing principles that we have discussed so far include:

Maverick Millionaire—maverick rich.

Motivation—inspiration.

Give—receive.

Effort—result.

Accountability—power.

Risk—reward.

Investment—dividend.

Internal affirmation—external realization.

Profound philosophies in every culture have been built upon the foundation of balanced opposites: yin and yang, good and evil, male and female, life and death...the list is endless. The Golden Rule (a version of which is found in every major world religion) is about balance.

Even science has come to hold balance as one of nature's fundamental ordering principles. Newton's second law about "equal and opposite reactions" was only the beginning; today's quantum physics takes this principle of balance to a whole new level. Look into an electron microscope and you'll observe that every material thing around us, and even our own physical selves, are composed of nothing but the chase and play–the *balance*–of positive and negative electrons!

Balancing Your Own Life

Achieving balance in our personal and professional lives is a great art. It begins with embracing the proper values and holding them in the proper scale. As we've talked about all along, we help ourselves by helping others. What other meaning could be held by that old business success formula, "find a hole and fill it"?

Personal balance means having the insight and the patience to put first things first…to walk before we run, and run before we fly. In realistic terms, this comes down to building a solid foundation for ourselves, before we begin to attempt great things. The truth of this idea was vividly dramatized for me when I attended a seminar by taught Brian Buffini, a dynamic speaker and owner of a success coaching company.

During his talk, Brian used a simple physical model to symbolize the progressive nature of what he called "the three levels of achievement: stability, success, and significance." He said we must pursue them one at a time, and achieve them in that order, in order to build a balanced, stable life.

First, he took a large bowl, a medium-sized bowl, and a small bowl, and stacked them vertically–one inside the other. The large bowl was on the bottom and contained the other bowls.

Next, Brian created a three-tiered tower structure by placing a medium box under the medium bowl and a small box under the small bowl. This tower structure, Brian explained, represents your life:

- The smallest bowl (on top) stands for the smallest level of ambition and values, which he called "stability"–having a job and a home; being able to make your payments on time; building up a decent credit rating; accumulating some experience and capital reserves.
- In the middle of the tower stood the medium-sized bowl, which Brian said stood for "success." Under the success category, Brian included such values as a fine home, a nice car, good clothes, perhaps owning your own business, and the wherewithal to enjoy more than the "bare minimum necessary" of the small-bowl items.
- At the bottom was the largest bowl, which Brian said stood for "significance." Brian defined "significance" as having the capability to take actions with a wide impact that goes beyond your own personal life, your family and your employees. "Significance," he said, "is about everyone else, not you!"

Brian began pouring water in the smallest, uppermost bowl, just as we might pour energy into achieving a basic level of stability–income, a home, and so on. When the small, top bowl became full, the water began to run over and spill downward.

The overflow was handily caught in the second, medium-sized bowl–"success." The point was that when you have accumulated enough ability, reserves, and energy in the "stability" category, the overflow will naturally power your drive to success.

When the middle (medium-sized) "success" bowl began to run over, the overflow ran smoothly into the largest, bottom bowl–"significance." In the same way, establishing the resources that come with success can give us a sound platform from which to exercise the larger influence over our environment that amounts to significance. "But when people pour into a bowl before the overflow, success or significance is left out," Brian cautioned.

For example, when Bill and Melinda Gates are able to devote part of their fortune to launch a foundation that takes the lead in eliminating polio from the global population, that is *significance!*

But the examples need not be so grandiose, and they don't necessarily have to be confined to charitable endeavors. Significance can mean influence on friends, family, neighbors, co-workers, and members of the local community. It can mean influence on society, art, government, religion.

Having dreams and ambition is a great thing, when we pursue them wisely. However, Brian Buffini explained that too many people allow their impatience to stampede them into making extremely unwise choices. These folks are so anxious to be much further down the road that they refuse to begin at the beginning. Before establishing a solid foundation (stability), they start pouring all their energy, time, and money into attempting success or significance. But without achieving the stability level first, they have few resources to put into those bigger "bowls."

As a result, the structure of their lives can easily come crashing down–because they never anchored themselves in stability before attempting success, or established a foundation of success before attempting significance. A slow and steady plan that begins at the beginning can bring a patient person, step by step, to success...long before an impatient, "start at the top" schemer finally arrives there.

It Is What It Is!

A powerful factor that helps us achieve balance is *accepting reality.* Sounds obvious, doesn't it? After all, few of us walk outside, look at the sky, trees, and grass and say: "Hmm, I don't like this reality. I think I'll change it. I'm going to have a green sky, purple trees, and orange grass."

Actually, many of us DO attempt to reorder reality all the time, only in a less-obvious way. For example, very young people may refuse to accept the simple truth that a certain person simply doesn't want to be involved with us at this time. Instead of accepting this fact and moving on, we scheme and sweat over how to "make" the person like us. Older people often laugh at this, but they repeat the same basic behavior on another level when they refuse to accept, for example, that they are no longer capable of performing certain actions as well as they used to.

An even worse example of refusing to accept reality, is inability to come to terms with the past...and get over it. How many people have we all seen wasting months and years of their lives, fretting and obsessing over a relationship or a business venture that failed six months ago? A year ago? Three years ago?

You cannot live in the past. It's a place that doesn't exist. But that doesn't stop legions of people from trying! These unhappy people don't like their current reality and refuse to accept it, so they waste precious time in sighs, regrets, recriminations, and what-ifs. They are living in the past, which means they're really living nowhere.

One more symptom of refusing to accept reality is when people often look at a certain fact or result, and spend a great deal of time and effort trying to understand "why" it is the way it its. Now, learning from our mistakes is an invaluable exercise, the essence of the School of Hard Knocks. But notice, our mistakes flow from our actions, which by definition are something we can control. It's another thing entirely, and quite useless, to spin our wheels asking "why" the outside universe is a certain way–particularly if you know ahead of time that you cannot do a thing to change it.

It's shocking how many otherwise-smart leaders in various fields–business, politics, education, you name it–waste time, energy, and resources trying to figure out "why" the universe is a certain way, in the deluded hope that they can "fix" it.

To take a concrete example from the business world, it's one thing to say, "This marketing campaign failed to get our message out." It's quite another thing to say, "If most people hate the super-sweet taste of our new soft drink, what can we say to them that will MAKE them like it?"

To this question, a wise leader responds: "Rather than trying to force consumers to like something they hate, accept the reality of the situation and put your energy into something productive. Such as, go find out what sort of beverage they do like and give that product to them, instead!"

This lesson was brought home to me with great force by my first and most influential mentor, Bill. He employs a simple but meaningful phrase that sums up a profound philosophy of accepting reality: "It is what it is."

Another way of expressing it is the truth voiced by generations of wise farmers (and pilots): "You can't argue with the weather."

As a CEO, I keep my balance by accepting reality–even when I don't like it. When the numbers are bad, it is what it is! I can't change what already happened. I can't change the facts of lost revenues when a deal falls out, or when some other negative event occurs. What happened, happened.

Taking this attitude has one big advantage: it puts the past behind me. It enables me to say: "Now let's move forward and fix the underlying issue so it doesn't happen again."

Accepting reality brings me another big advantage: serenity. Most people recognize the first line of *The Serenity Prayer* by Reinhold Niebuhr.

God grant me the serenity
to accept the things I cannot change;
courage to change the things I can;
and wisdom to know the difference.

Fewer people are as familiar with the second verse, but it's equally powerful–and you don't need to be any sort of religious believer to catch the poem's spirit of "It is what it is!" The second verse goes on to recommend "Living one day at a time, Enjoying one moment at a time," and "Accepting hardships as the pathway to peace." The author urges us to accept that this world is "not as I would have it," yet to realize that through acceptance, we can learn to be "happy in this life."

And we can learn to be effective and successful, too.

Balancing Today Against Tomorrow; Balancing Pleasure Against Pain

I've spoken many times in this book about the need to delay gratification in order to stay on track and achieve our goals. This is a form of balance: we are trading off today's enjoyment against tomorrow's achievement. It doesn't mean giving up all pleasure or enjoyment. It just means that balancing the needs of today against the rewards of tomorrow, is the best way to make sure those rewards really do become a part of our lives.

Sometimes, it may be necessary to go beyond just delaying gratification, and move all the way into enduring a certain amount of discomfort or even worse. Athletes have a saying: "No pain, no gain." Steve Prefontaine, the legendary international track star, once explained the reason he was so confident that he would win every race. "I can endure more pain than anybody," he said.

The same principle applies to the field of business. Jeff Jonas dropped out of high school to follow his dream of inventing great new computer software. He paid a high price for this decision. By age of 19, he had racked up debts of more than $100,000 and he was living out of his car. But he stuck with his dream, saying virtually the same thing as Steve Prefontaine about his will to win: "I have a phenomenal ability to endure pain!" By 2005, he sold his groundbreaking company SRD to IBM for many millions of dollars. And he's still working hard and playing hard at what he loves most: creating innovative new software.

The pain of short-term sacrifice is endurable when it's balanced against the expectation, faith, and knowledge that in the future, we will be rewarded by seeing our dreams become realities.

The Balance of Work & Play; The Balance of Mind & Body

Balance also extends to our physical selves. If you're healthy inside, you're healthy outside (and vice versa). I feel better on a daily basis, and am more productive, when I work out and treat my body right, and when I meditate. A sound mind, a purpose-driven life, solid values, can improve your physical health and your success.

I have found that most ultra-successful business professionals, and certainly the billionaires, have a fitness and diet regimen. They eat right. They exercise regularly. Many of those who don't ensure such balance in their lives, eventually get the message in various ways. J.W. Marriott Jr., CEO of Marriott International Incorporated, knows. "By the third heart attack, I concluded that if cardiovascular trouble didn't kill me, my wife Donna probably would if I didn't make some changes in the way I was living," Marriott admitted.

J.W. not only adopted a fitness regiment, he also ate better, got more sleep, delegated more, learned to say "no" to excessive demands on his time, and broadened his focus beyond the job. "One of the most valuable lessons that my heart attacks taught me," he said, "is to improve the balance of my life between work and play. If this sounds like an odd goal, you're probably never suffered from chronic workaholism."

It's easier to let the cares of the office slip away when you're absorbed in a good swim, a horseback ride, painting your latest landscape, or tickling the ivories in a jam session with friends. And from personal experience, I can attest that the view from 10,000 feet makes your business problems look very small and unimportant!

Fitness is important to me. I do four or five workouts a week. I recently began an early morning workout program. I get up at 6AM. I go to the gym, lift weights, then get on the cardio machine for 10-30 minutes, go home and shower, then drink a protein shake.

I do a brief period of meditation at that point. If the weather is pleasant I sit outside and enjoy the environment. Then I go to work. By 10 or 11AM, I find my day has already been very productive. Frequently, I put in 8 to 14 hour days, depending on the flow of work. But when I finally come home, I can truly relax and enjoy myself, knowing that I've put in a good day's effort for *myself* as well as for my business. (I love my business, but I never confuse the two!)

The reason balance is such a powerful principle is that it means cooperating with the laws of nature. The wind and the waves are on the side of the ablest navigator; gravity and weather seem to favor the ablest aviator.

Cause and effect are a universal law. What you give, you receive, is a universal law. What you believe, you achieve, is a universal law. What you visualize, you magnetize, is a universal law.

You can make these laws work for you—achieving a state of balance that means you sail through life—or, you can work against them, ignoring the warning signs that disaster is imminent.

What we yearn after, we become. When we yearn to be in harmony with the laws of nature, we *become* those laws. Plant yourself firmly on the side of universal law, and you'll surprise yourself with what great things can happen…seemingly effortlessly.

For the man or woman who has mastered this principle, what is there that we cannot hope for?

Anything, truly *anything*, is possible for us!

Chapter 28:

The Most Important Job You'll Ever Have

I know of an extremely successful executive we'll call Jim Matthews (not his real name). As it happens, Jim owns his own business. But his story applies to every single one of us—whether we own a business, run a business, work for somebody else, work for ourselves, or even if you don't happen to be working at all right now because you're a student, a new parent, or for some other reason.

Jim is a Maverick Millionaire. He's a hard-working, creative, funny, optimistic guy. As a team leader he is inspiring, always encouraging everyone around him to believe that "We can do it!" Jim sets high standards. He demands the best from his staff, but he is also more than fair with each person he deals with. He is generous with his time and concern, quick to pass out praise and credit for a job well done.

Jim's partners and employees love him. His clients and his suppliers love him, too. Not all of his competitors love him, but that's to be expected–Jim constantly beats their pants off.

Jim is also rich outside. With fewer than 100 employees, The Matthews Company bills its nationwide client base for an annual sum that has many, many zeroes in it. Jim's state and national associations have elected him their president more than once. As a visionary communicator and "get things done" kind of guy, he is one of his industry's most respected leaders.

Does Jim Matthews have any flaws? Unfortunately, yes. And it's a big one.

At many companies, the group dynamic resembles a certain type of dysfunctional family. No matter how beautifully the rest of the team gets along, one person somehow ends up becoming the "designated scapegoat." Whenever anything goes wrong, the scapegoat inevitably gets most of the blame, fairly or unfairly. The scapegoat is constantly singled out for on-the-job mistakes, regardless of whether they're minor, trivial, or unavoidable. The scapegoat may even be the target of harsh, *personal* criticism.

Regrettably, this is the case at The Matthews Company. As I mentioned, most people at the company are expected to live up to very strict performance standards. At the same time, they also receive plenty of encouragement, and are given many opportunities to improve. When a mistake is made, Jim occasionally gets mad. Usually, however, he remains calm, because in most instances he knows the person was trying their best. His typical response is to take the person aside and calmly say, "Okay, we both realize that didn't work out. Now, let me show you a better approach. Try it this way next time, and I'm sure you'll succeed."

However, Jim tolerates a shocking disparity between this norm (almost always positive) and the way one particular person is treated (relentlessly negative). In fact, the "designated scapegoat" at The Matthews Company is constantly harangued with messages such as: "You moron! How could you have made such a stupid mistake! Don't you realize you're costing the company money? What the hell's the matter with you? Why don't you THINK for a change?"

Who is the unlucky target of this relentless stream of negativity?

Why doesn't the poor slob just quit?

Ironically, the scapegoat at The Matthews Company would never dream of resigning...because he is president and CEO, Jim Matthews. What's more, the party who unloads this steady stream of abuse is, you guessed it, Jim Matthews.

Some years ago, *Newsweek* published a cover story on stress. At the heart of the article were three lists:

(1) The Top Ten Stress-Causing Jobs In America.

(2) The Top Ten Symptoms Of Severe Stress.

(3) The Top Ten Coping Mechanisms To Beat Stress.

On his worst months, Jim suffered nine of the ten symptoms on the first list. He had insomnia; gut problems (ulcers, indigestion, colitis, etc.); skin problems (hives, eczema, psoriasis, tics, itching); muscle spasms, muscle injuries, and chronic muscular tension (even though he never lifts anything heavier than a suitcase); circulation issues (high blood pressure, chest pains); depressed immune system (leading to frequent colds and flus); emotional issues (depression, irritability, temper tantrums–always directed at himself); social isolation (he traveled much more than he needs to, in order to avoid dealing with relationships at home); and he suffered from being accident-prone. The only symptom Jim didn't have is number ten, short-term memory loss.

(According to *Newsweek*, the three top stress-causing jobs in America, in ascending order, are: number three, taxi driver. Number two, police officer. And what is the number-one, top stress-causing job in America? Public schoolteacher! What do they have in common? The formula for stress, *Newsweek* explained, boils down to "lots of responsibility, no authority."

> **MAVERICK MOTIVATOR:**
>
> Don't compare yourself to your parents. American Sociological Association researchers found that by age 30, only 46 percent of women and 31 percent of men have finished school, left home, gotten married, had a child or reached financial independence than did their counterparts in 1960.

I agree with this formula, as far as it goes. But I believe that's only half the equation. Stress can be created just as well by reversing the formula's elements, as in Jim's case: lots of authority, no responsibility. Not that Jim lacks burdens and obligations—he has plenty of those. However, Jim does not *exercise true responsibility toward himself.*

Think about it. If you owned a dog, say a sheep dog on a working farm…would you constantly berate the dog? Would you kick the dog every time one sheep left the fold? Even if the dog quickly nudged the sheep back into the right pasture? Would you deprive the dog of company, encouragement, and affection? Would you refuse to pet the dog? Would you make the dog sleep in a pet kennel every other week, so that it rarely enjoyed the emotional comfort of a stable, nurturing home environment?

Of course not!

If you saw someone treating a dog in this deplorable fashion, would you say he was a responsible pet owner? Again, of course not. Which means, the Jim Matthews of the world are guilty of treating themselves in a way that–literally–shouldn't happen to a dog.

You Have a Relationship With Yourself

Jim's story turned around when a close friend approached him once with the idea that he needed to work on his relationship with himself. At first, Jim was baffled by this suggestion. "How can I have a relationship with myself?" he asked.

The friend explained that Jim needed to mentally "step outside of himself" and look upon himself the same way that he looked at his employees—or, for that matter, the same way that Jim looked at his brother (a much less successful, much less hardworking business owner in the same city). Jim treated all these people with kindness and encouragement. He needed to see that he was not in a special class by himself–neither blessed with godlike powers that demanded superhuman perfection, nor cursed with inherent depravity that justified relentless self-punishment. Instead, Jim owed the same simple, decent consideration to himself that he automatically granted to everyone else in his life.

In other words, Jim needed to see himself objectively and treat himself with *kindness, caring,* and most of all, *responsibility.*

Simple as that sounds, this concept proved a great revelation for Jim. Gradually, he learned to view himself almost as though he were two different people. He was both management and labor of a single enterprise, a unique human "corporation" that might be described as "Jim Matthews, Inc." In this capacity, Jim was both supervisor and worker... teacher and student...observer and doer.

Over the next couple of years, Jim put this insight into practice. As his relationship with himself improved, slowly but steadily, his symptoms began to disappear one by one. His blood pressure went down. His stomach ulcers healed. He was able to sleep longer and more soundly. The skin on his face and hands cleared up. He cut back on travel, found more time for friends and family. Most important, Jim's internal mood improved. He showed the same sunny face to himself in the mirror, that he had always showed to the outside world. He was a far happier–and in my view, a far more successful–person.

Jim learned a crucial lesson that is invaluable for all of us: *you have a relationship with yourself.* You are the "manager" of yourself–the manager of your inner resources. I said at the beginning of this book that the nexus between being "rich inside" and "rich outside" is learning to leverage your inner resources. This relationship between yourself as the person who does the leveraging, and the person who is "being leveraged," is the crucial connection between the two kinds of wealth, inner and outer.

Again, this is true regardless of whether you're a business owner or an employee; a technician, a clerk, or a manager; in the workforce or out of it. And it will be true your entire life. Your relationship with yourself is the *most important relationship* you'll ever have. And, being your own manager is the *most important job* you'll ever have.

Learn to think of yourself as both the CEO and, quite separately, as the sole employee of "YOU, Inc." Do your best to make sure the two "you's" get along! To give "YOU, Inc." the best possible chance of becoming rich outside, first be rich inside–*then leverage those inner resources with the same love and compassion for yourself that you would naturally give to anybody who works for you or with you.*

Taking a responsible attitude toward this "most important job" of self-management brings invaluable benefits:

- ¢ By cultivating your relationship with yourself…by creating a healthy and nurturing self-relationship…you instantly triple the value of being "rich inside."
- ¢ In addition, you vastly increase your odds of becoming "rich outside." This is true because a person who is a "house divided against himself" is not getting the full value out of his inner resources; whereas there's no stopping a person who is enthusiastically "on his own team."
- ¢ Finally, by cultivating a healthy relationship with yourself, you help ensure that achieving inner and outer wealth adds up to the final goal of life: real happiness.

When was the last time you told that person in the mirror, "You're terrific"? You have what it takes. We make a great team, you and I. Together, we're going to WIN!"

Chapter 29:

Putting it all Together

The time has come to take inventory of what we've learned. The Maverick Millionaire principles are not a laundry list of discrete ideas for "making it." On the contrary: taken as a whole, these principles blend into a single, comprehensive roadmap to making your life everything you want it to be. In this chapter, I want to show the organic connection that links all of the principles discussed so far, synthesizing them into a unified, powerful vision for your journey to health, wealth, and happiness.

If Success Is a Journey, Desire Is the Fuel...

A concentrated overview of these principles must start with desire, the ultimate secret of success. Each person's definition of success is–and should be–as individual as your fingerprint. Only by pursuing your most passionate longings, only by seeking to fulfill your heart's deepest desire, will you find what it takes inside yourself to remain on your quest: energy and inspiration.

Desire is the fuel of achievement. When we allow our real desires to lead us, they generate a constant flow of that energy and inspiration–the ultimate "renewable resource."

Being a Maverick Millionaire includes getting comfortable with the fact that we desire wealth. Being rich outside almost always means focusing on the goal of *financial success as an end in itself.*

It's perfectly okay to want to be wealthy; and it's absolutely vital to face up to the price of achieving that goal, including the decision to invest our time and resources in the most productive directions. Often, this means delaying gratification time and again, until our goal is attained. It also means learning to love our work, preferably by finding the work that we truly do love and were meant to do.

Goals Are the Milestones

If desire is the ultimate fuel of achievement, then goals are the milestones on the road to success. Achieving a goal has a spiritual, not just a practical, meaning. It is a fundamentally creative act, not merely an act of willpower and self-discipline. Achieving a goal is creative because it means transferring an idea from inside your head to the physical world. *Writing down your goals* can be a wonderful tool to begin transferring dreams from inside to outside.

Action is how we push down on the accelerator in our drive for success. The key to successful action is to start small and build momentum. Gaining knowledge and confidence as we go, we can progress from small actions (such as writing down a goal) to larger actions (such as creating a business plan), then to still larger actions (such as starting a company, opening an office, hiring a staff).

Growth is a natural, organic process. Continual learning in the school of real-life experience is a reward that we win by participating in this process, not a price we pay. Our path can be smoothed considerably if we find an experienced mentor to offer wisdom and guidance. Mentors, too, are usually found through an organic process of friendship, not by aggressively recruiting a candidate as if you were hiring someone for an important "job." You compensate your mentor for his time and expertise, by giving whole-heartedly of your respect and appreciation.

In a similar vein, every single relationship you have in your life–whether in business, the social realm, or in cultural or government circles–is built on some sort of transaction. Every relationship is built on give and take or "mutual giving."

Realizing this, we can easily see why the best business deals (and the best transactions in every sphere of life) are win-win scenarios. Both parties benefit equally, or nearly equally, from a great deal or a healthy transaction. Both parties are thus empowered and incentivized to come back for more deals or transactions. That ranges from deals you make with your own team, to deals you make with customers and suppliers. A good manager's attitude toward his employees is the same as a good negotiator's attitude toward his partner in a business deal: "By helping you, I help myself."

In this way, business relationships (and all other types of relationships) can also acquire the power of organic growth.

Service Is the Seed

The seed for this organic growth is planted in each new relationship by taking *an attitude of service toward* your potential friend, colleague, ally, client, or customer.

Service begins with the art of listening, which really means the powerful art of *validating the other person.* Such validation can grow through a process of continual evolution: from listening to dialog... from dialog into brainstorming (or negotiation, in the best sense of that term)...from brainstorming to "let's make a deal"...from deals to alliances...and from alliances to world-transforming enterprises and industries.

The ethic of service blossoms in many ways. One important form of service, even though many people do not think of it this way, is leadership. It has long been known that *the greatest leader of all, is the one who performs the greatest service of all.* In a business context, that means stepping back to achieve a "true CEO" perspective: focusing on what is good for the company as a whole.

A crucial function of leadership is creating mutually shared goals. But at the level of leadership, goals are not private; they are group commitments, group guidelines, and group endeavors. When such collective goals are achieved, they become group successes, too.

There are many ways to turn a company's theoretical objective into a team's genuine, living, breathing goal. All of them, however, seek to leverage the entire team's "inner resources" so that a group of individuals who are separately "rich inside," learn to blend their strengths so as to become collectively "rich outside."

One of the best ways to bring out your team's inner resources is also very simple: get 'em talking! This, above all, is what meetings are for. As the seed of a single relationship begins with "active listening" to one person, the seed of a group cohesion and teamwork begins with active listening to a roomful of people.

Growth–whether it's personal growth, or growing a business–means letting go of the old and embracing the new. This entails a certain degree of risk. Closely related to this is the need to make decisions, and the need to commit to those decisions in a meaningful way, once they are made.

Is there a cost involved? Certainly. But one of the greatest resources that makes a person a Maverick Millionaire is the love of adventure. This means learning to enjoy taking (educated, carefully considered) risks, and learning to find the psychological rewards in following a commitment through to its end.

The art of deciding which risks to take, and how to take them, is called *strategy*. A great strategy is not set in stone, but it is written down. A great strategist does not cling to every tactical guess, regardless of changing circumstances, but continually adapts and revises his plan to meet new conditions. The inner resource required here is balance–the ability to balance the (unchanging) big picture against the (constantly changing) day-to-day details.

Creativity is a wonderful inner resource that will make you externally wealthy. *The world's most severely under-utilized form of creativity is adjusting our own perceptual "filters" so that we see opportunities where others see only circumstances!* Negotiations and brainstorming are opportunities to find and express your creativity in the context of business relationships (or any other type of relationships).

See the pattern here? From start to finish, it's what is inside you–the inner Maverick Millionaire–not the outer circumstances you confront–which determine whether or not you become "maverick rich."

The good news? I am willing to bet that you already have desire, inspiration, an ethic of service, stick-to-it-iveness, the willingness to make decisions and take risks, and the creativity to see wonderful possibilities hidden in everyday, ordinary situations. If so, then you begin your journey to success with all the inner resources you will need.

You are *already* on your way…

Chapter 30:

You Gotta Believe!

There is a funny story behind this popular catchphrase. The motto caught on some years ago when the New York Mets were in sixth place in the National Baseball League pennant race.

Clearly, the team's record up to that point was "distinguished mainly by mediocrity." In the stadium, fans draped signs and banners with many encouraging messages ("We've Got Pennant Fever"), and a few less-encouraging ones ("The Mets Stink" and "NY Mets–Victims Of The Energy Crisis").

Hoping to rouse the team to greater efforts, the ball club's chairman of the board, M. Donald Grant, gave a locker-room pep talk to the players. According to some reports, Grant's speech was so full of "uplifting" clichés and hokum that when it was over, the relief pitcher, Tug McGraw–known for his impish sense of humor–started mocking Grant by yelling "He's right! He's right! Just believe! You gotta believe!"

The other players cracked up. In fact, they thought McGraw's corny sentiment was so side-splitting, they repeated it among themselves for days afterwards, usually with a belly laugh. "Believe! You just gotta believe!" Ha, ha, ha.

Well, there are worse things than laughing your way to victory. Somehow the team's performance began improving from that day. They moved up to fifth place. Then fourth. Then third. Then second. The players were still crying, "You gotta believe!"–but by now, it was no longer a joke.

That year, the New York Mets won the National League pennant. The press latched onto the slogan and it entered American popular culture. *You gotta believe!*

Now that you've arrived at the final chapter of this book, I can only say: welcome to the rest of your life! Perhaps you purchased *The Maverick Millionaire* hoping it would give you the secrets to success. By now, you realize that ultimately there are no real secrets. The universe is an open book. Life reveals its bedrock truths to any of us who look hard enough at the world…and who look deeply enough within ourselves.

I hope you feel this book has given you some tools that can help unlock your own potential. I've tried to address the realistic, down-to-earth issues that hold so many people back, allowing you to see that becoming a success is entirely possible. This is one fact that I know to be absolutely, one-thousand-percent true:

IF I CAN DO IT, YOU CAN DO IT!!!

At the same time, no book, seminar, correspondence course, or class will automatically make you a success. At first, this may seem like cause for dismay. Eventually, however, you will realize it's actually very good news...because it means *the power to make your life successful is in your own hands, mind, and heart.*

Only YOU can find and unlock those precious qualities within yourself...the qualities that make you a Maverick Millionaire.

Rather than trusting in shallow success formulas or pie-in-the-sky promises, place your faith and belief *in yourself*, and in the creative Higher Power or Process that brought all of us into being. If you have the patience to go prospecting for those inner resources within yourself, and if you have the patient determination to put those resources to work in the world, nothing can stop you.

At that moment, you'll make the most amazing discovery of all. The journey wasn't worthwhile because of that pot of gold at the end of the rainbow. Money and the trappings of wealth, after all, come and go.

The journey is worthwhile for what it teaches us about ourselves...for the disciplines and virtues that we cultivate on the way...for the person we become, while we're working to achieve our success.

"YOU GOTTA BELIEVE!"

Afterword

Becoming a Maverick Millionaire™

Now it's up to you!

And now–the time has come, as you always knew it would. Your airplane awaits you on the tarmac: sleek, gleaming, immaculate. High overhead, the blue sky beckons...welcoming you to try the air.

It's time to rise above the mundane world of the earthbound. Time to become the winged being in reality, that you always knew you were inwardly.

Time to transcend old limits and experience something new, daring, adventurous. At last, it's time to taste freedom, and breathe the air of limitless possibility.

Your flight instructors and your fellow pilots have taught you all they can. They know you have the skills, the desire, and the destiny to fly. You know it, too.

So now, it's up to you...

"There shall be wings!
...The spirit cannot die;
and man, who shall know all
...shall have wings..."

— Leonardo da Vinci